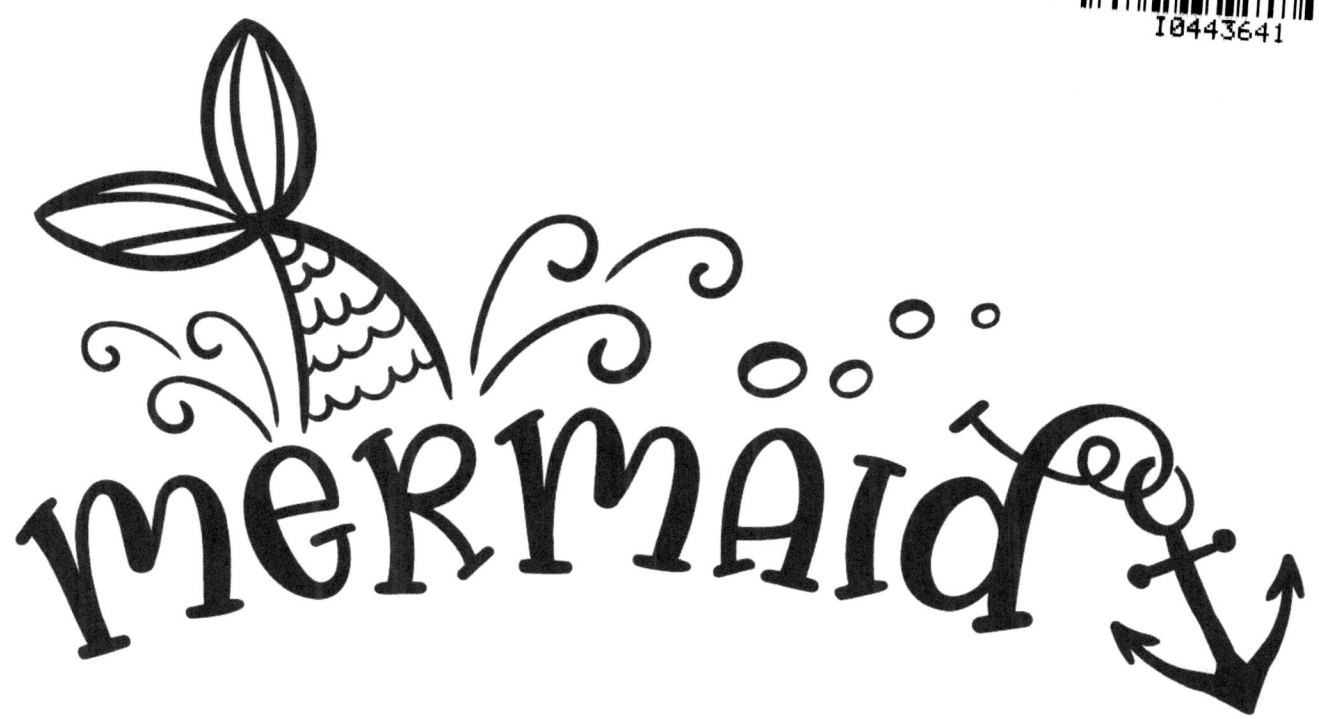

THIS BOOK BELONGS TO:

_____

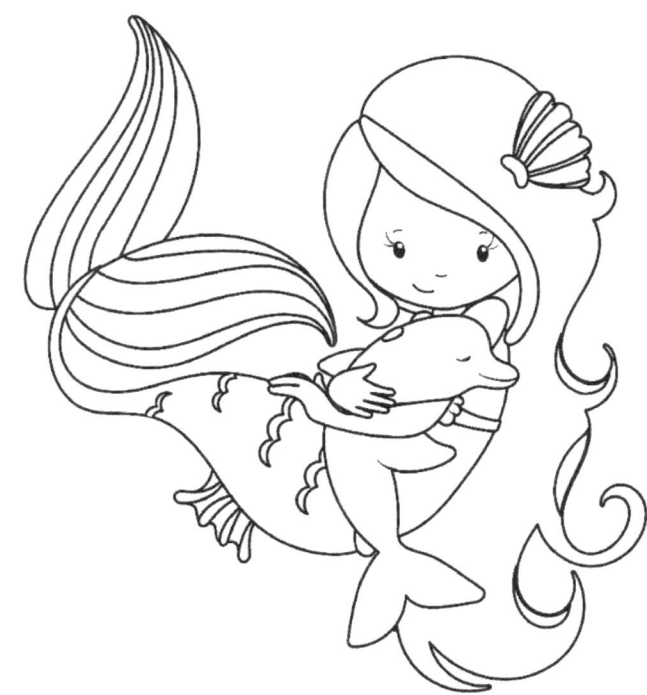

COLORING BOOK FOR GIRLS AGES 4-8

COPYRIGHT © SWEET PUZZLERS ALL RIGHT RESERVED.

TEST COLOR

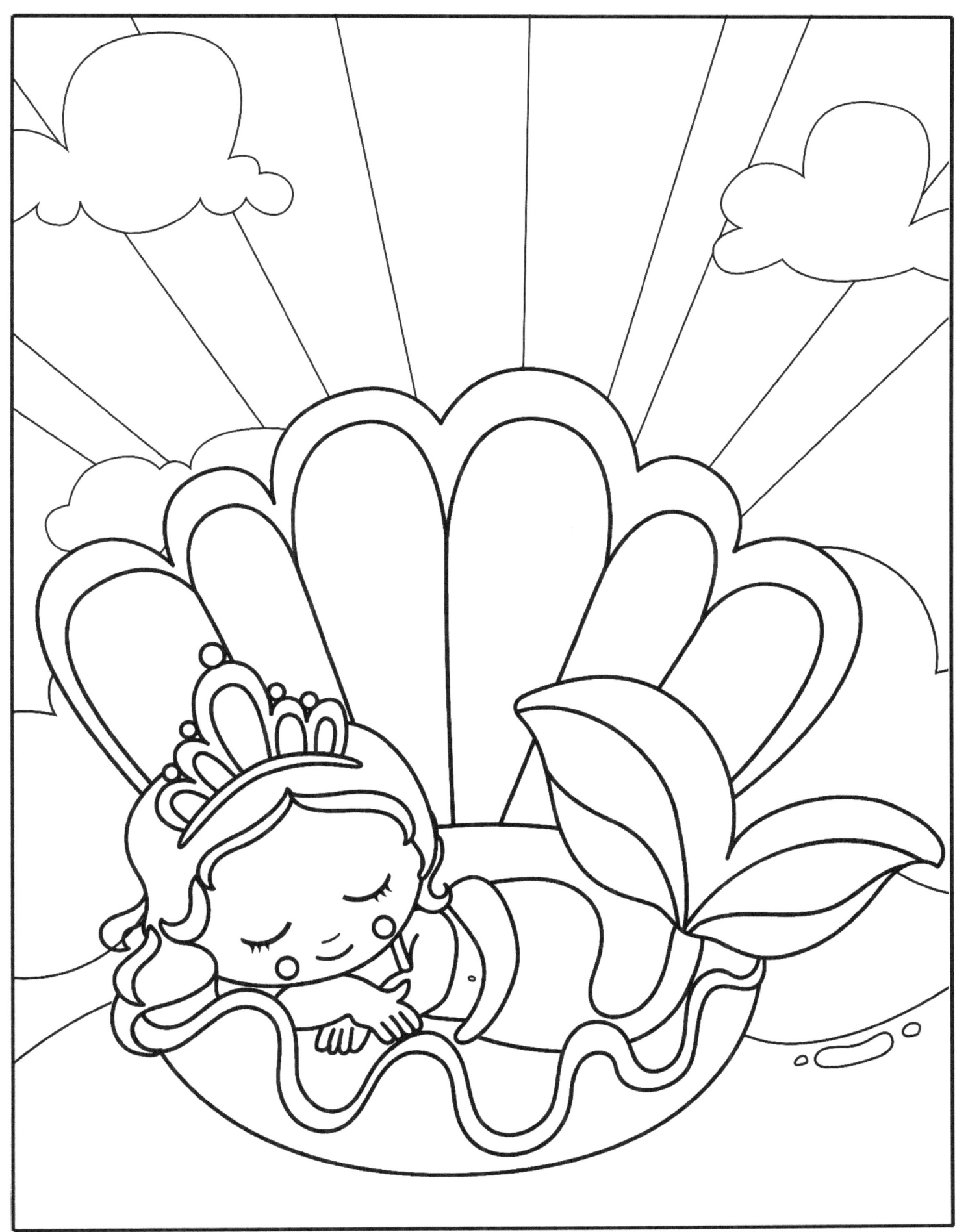

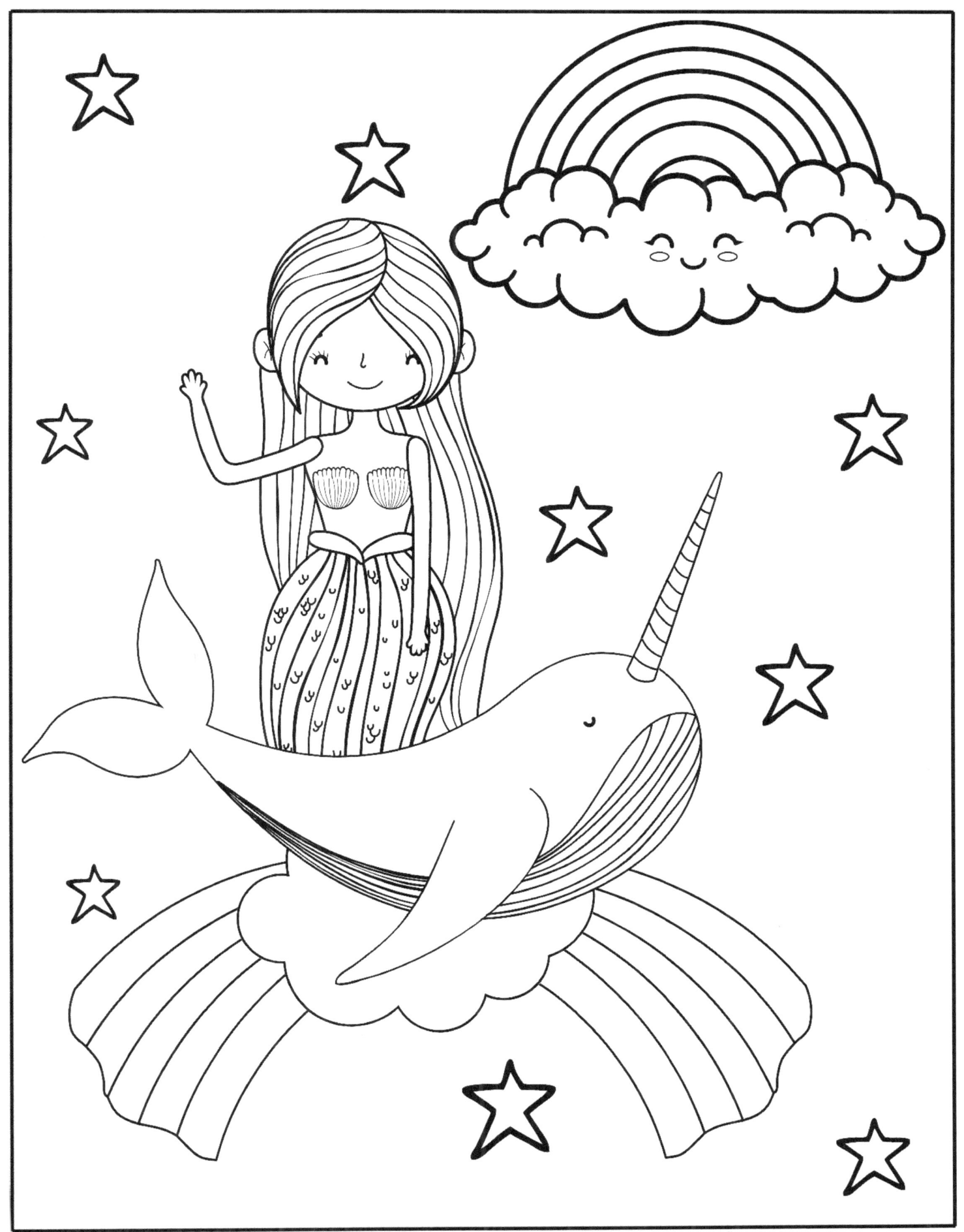

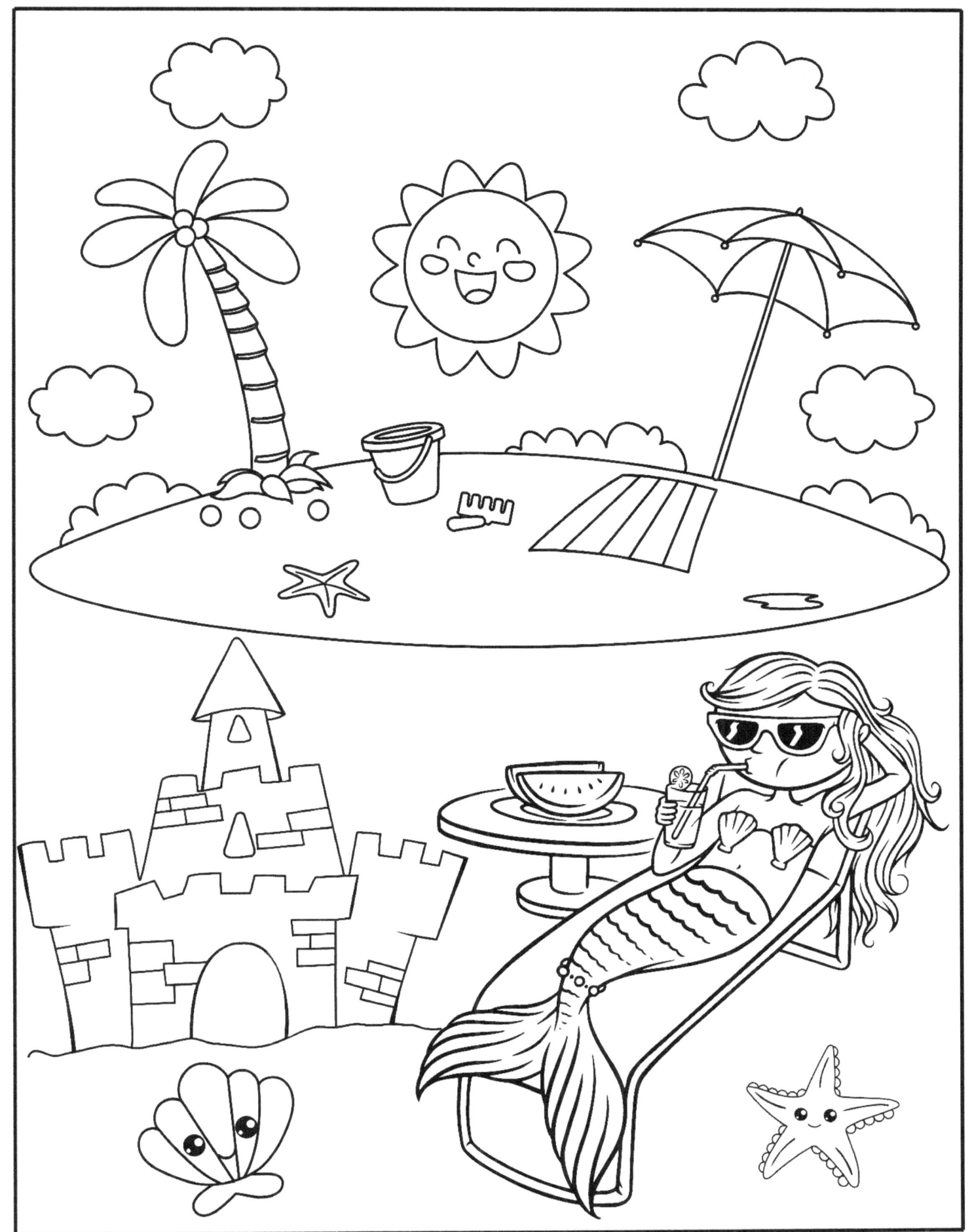

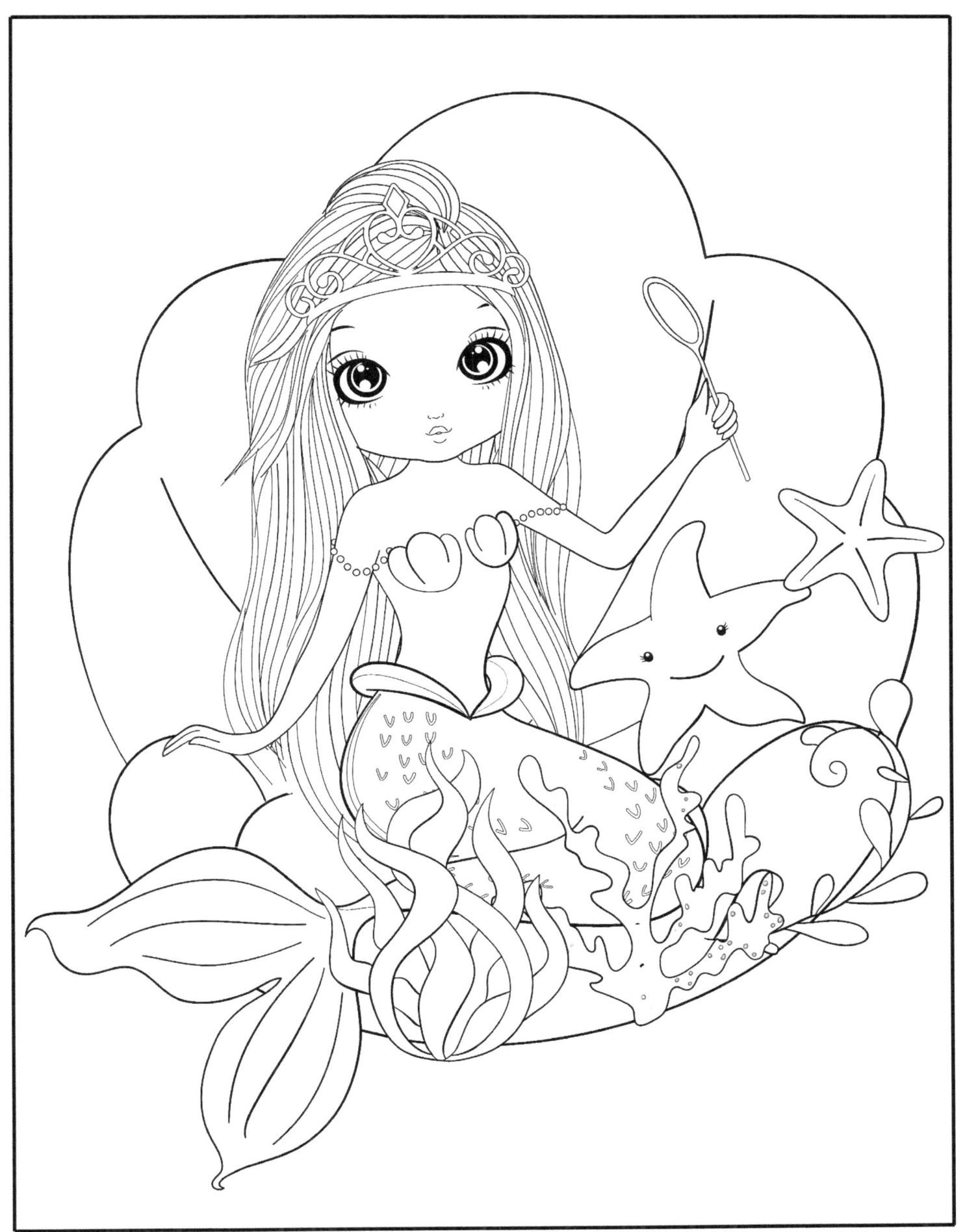

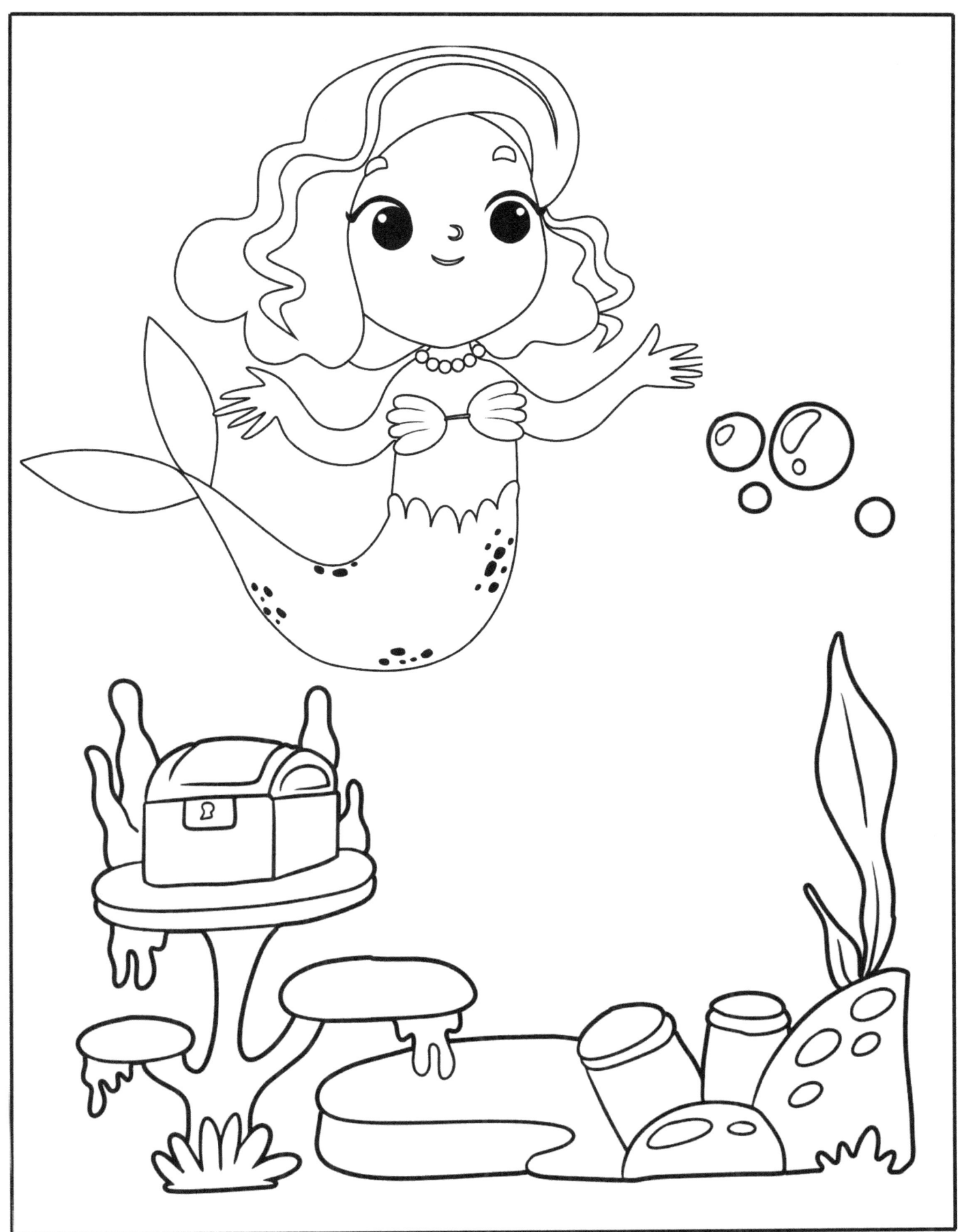

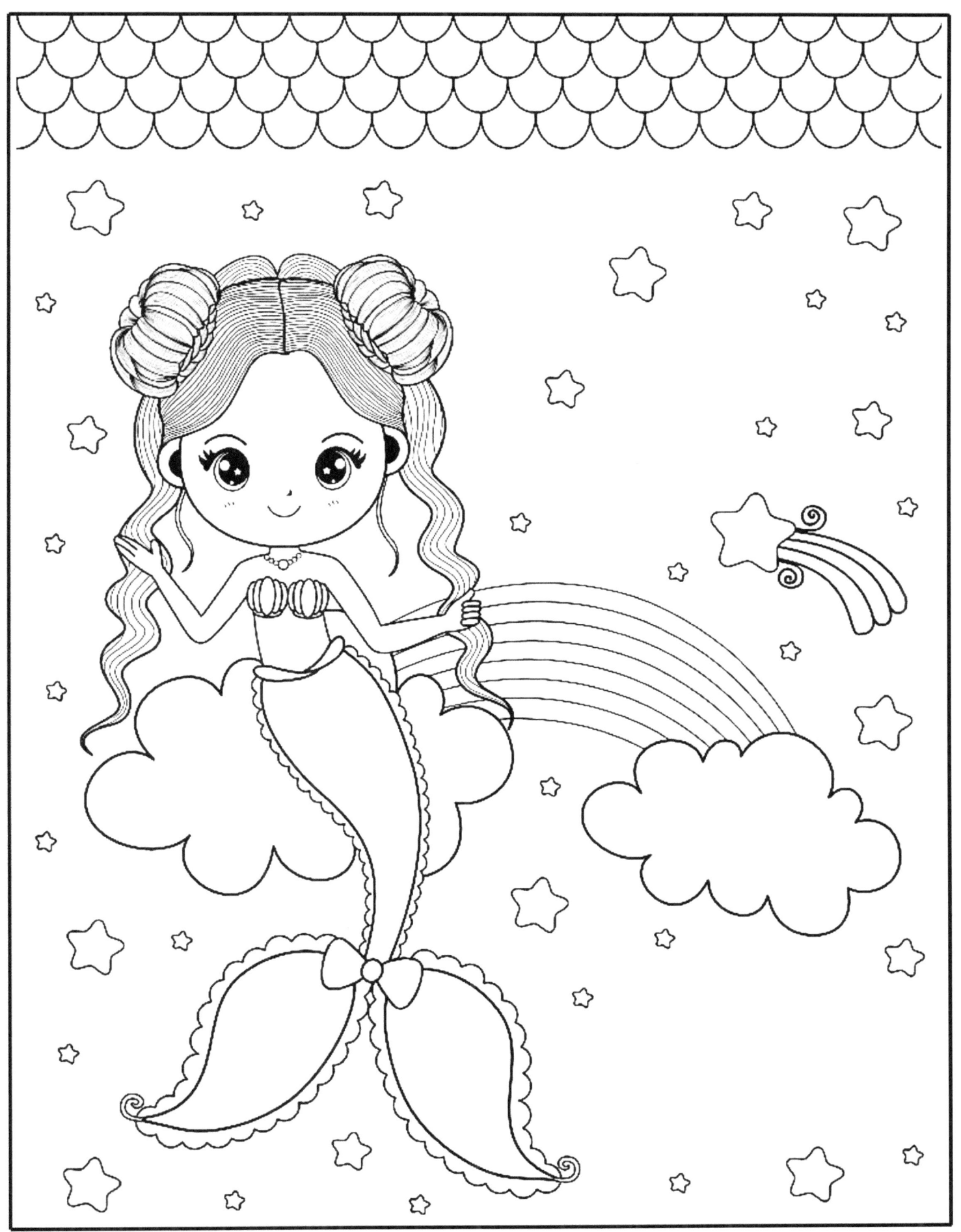

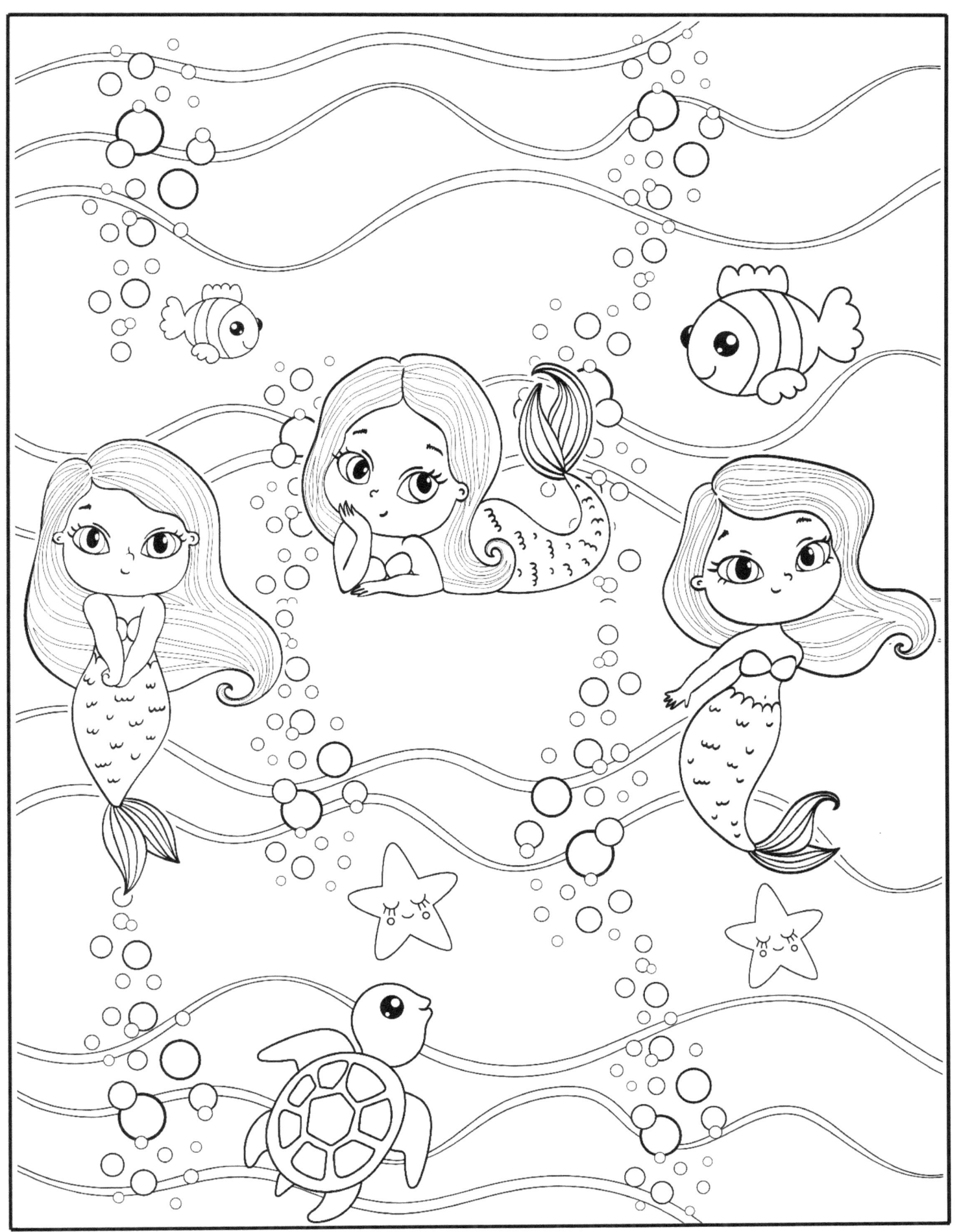

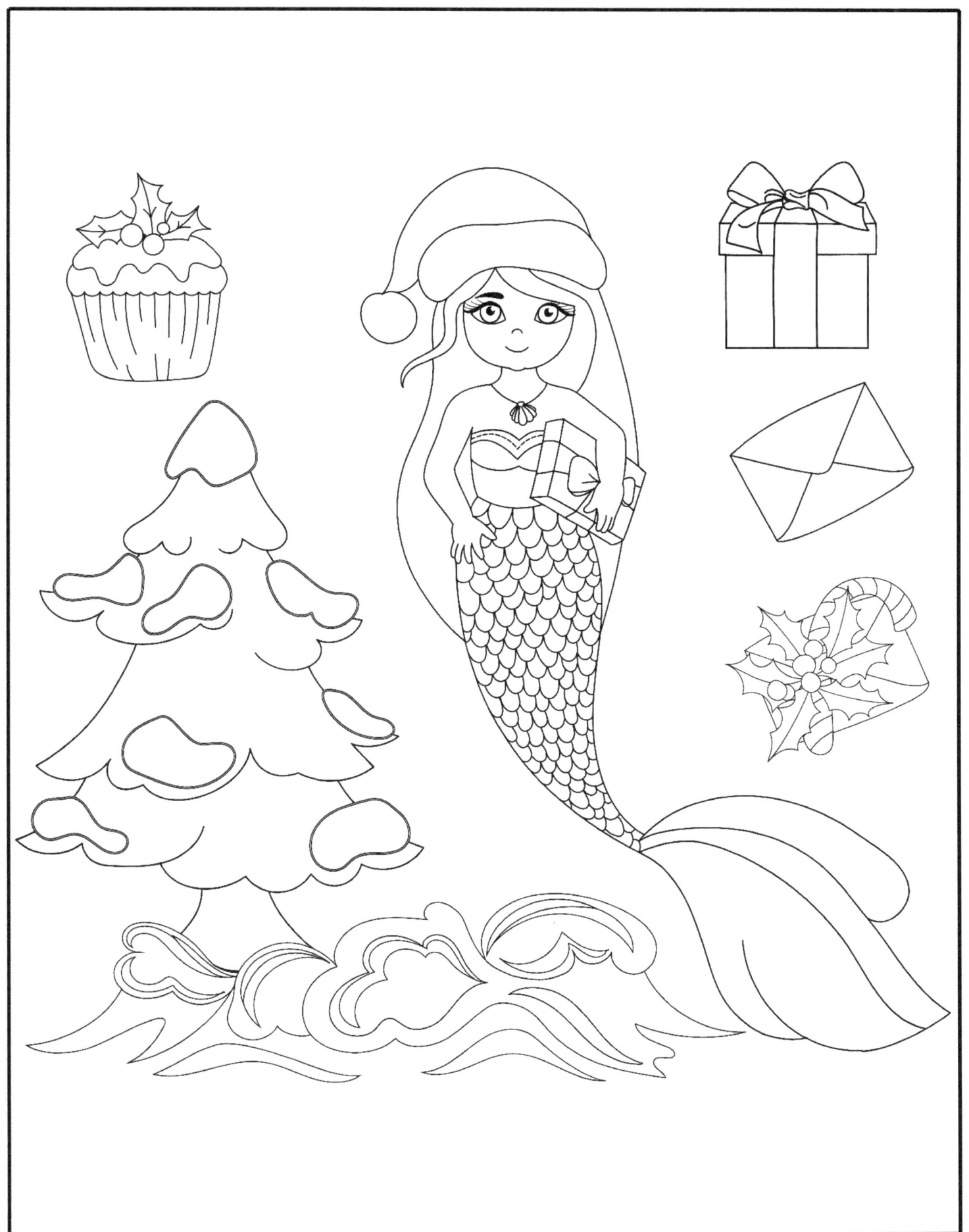

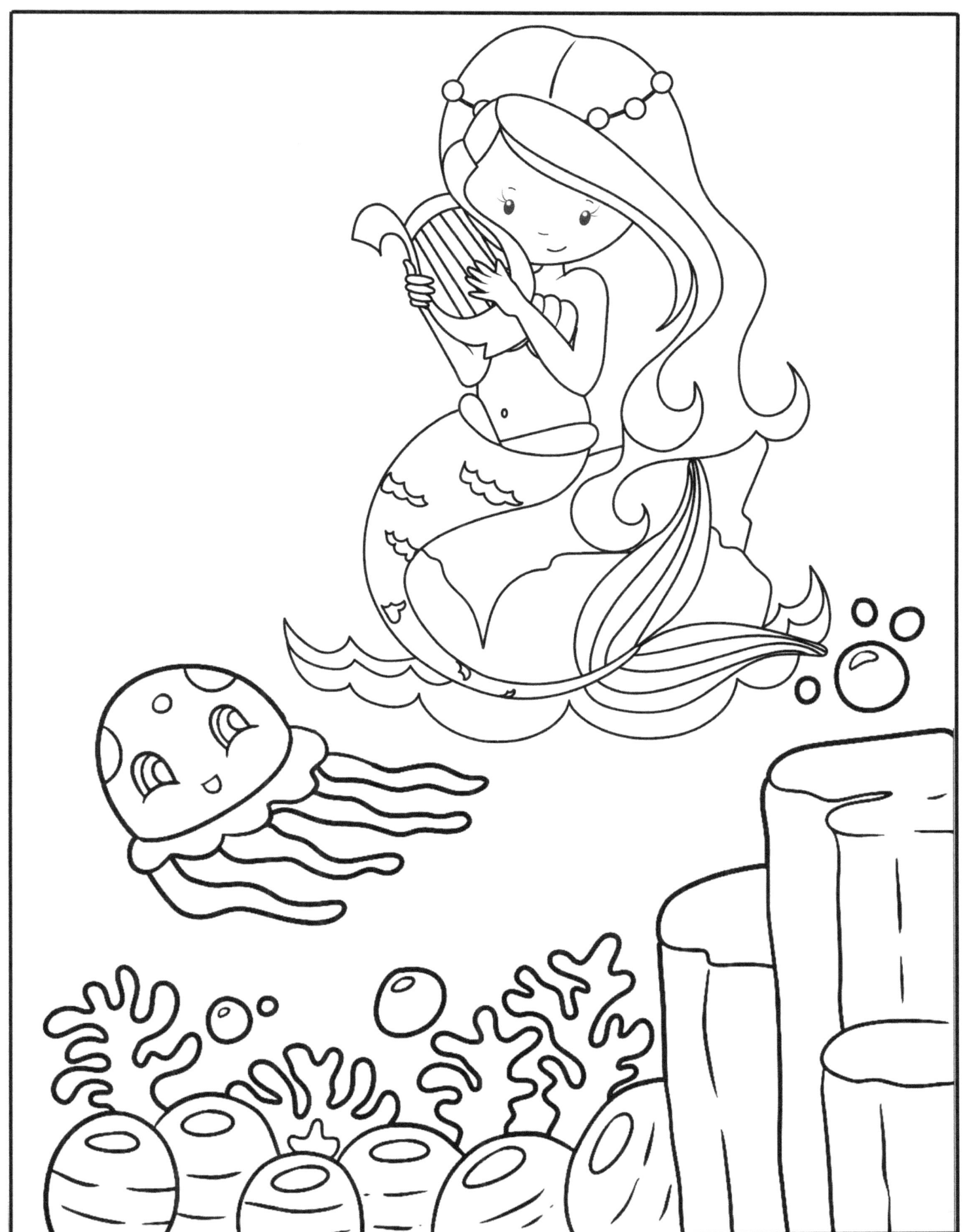

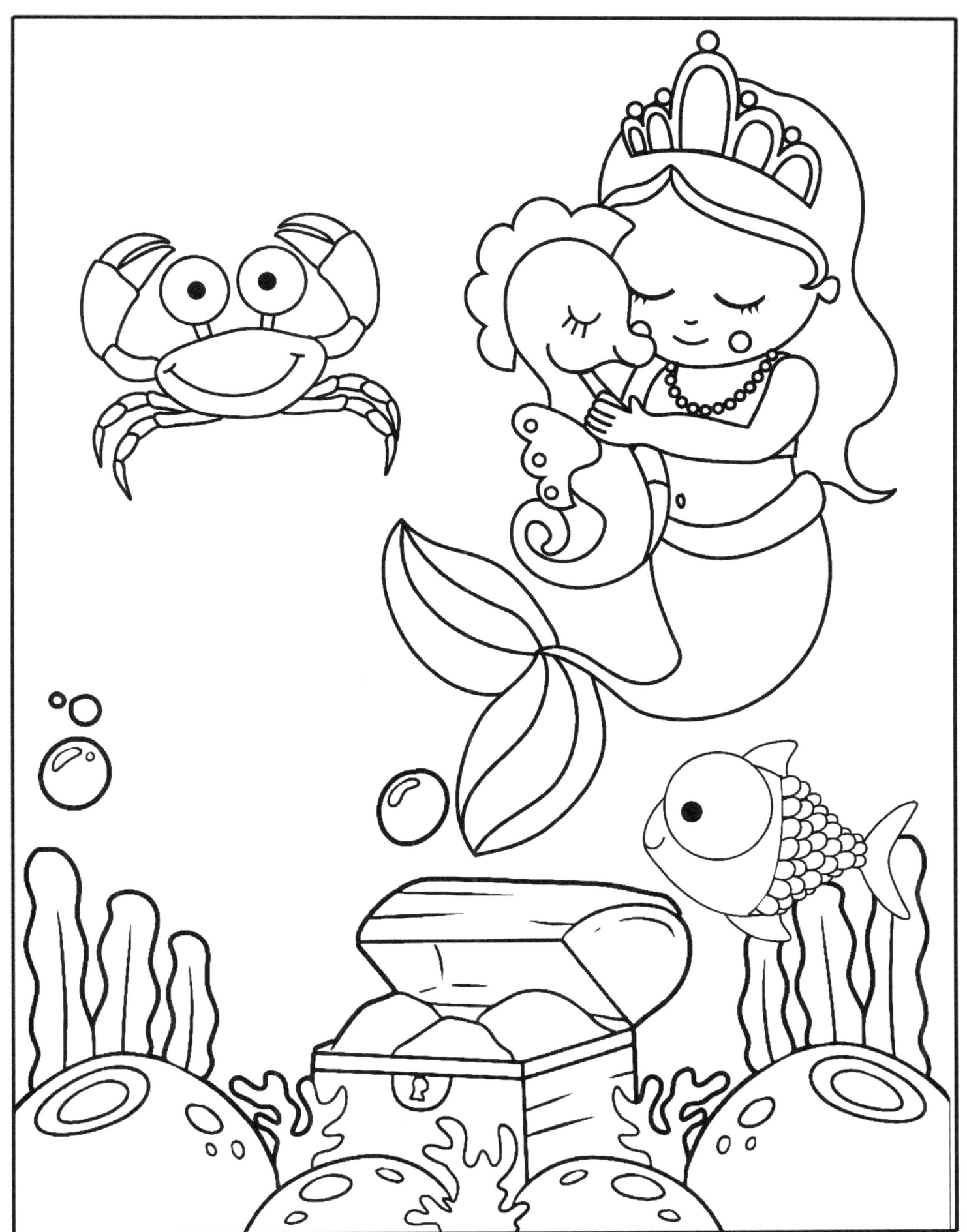

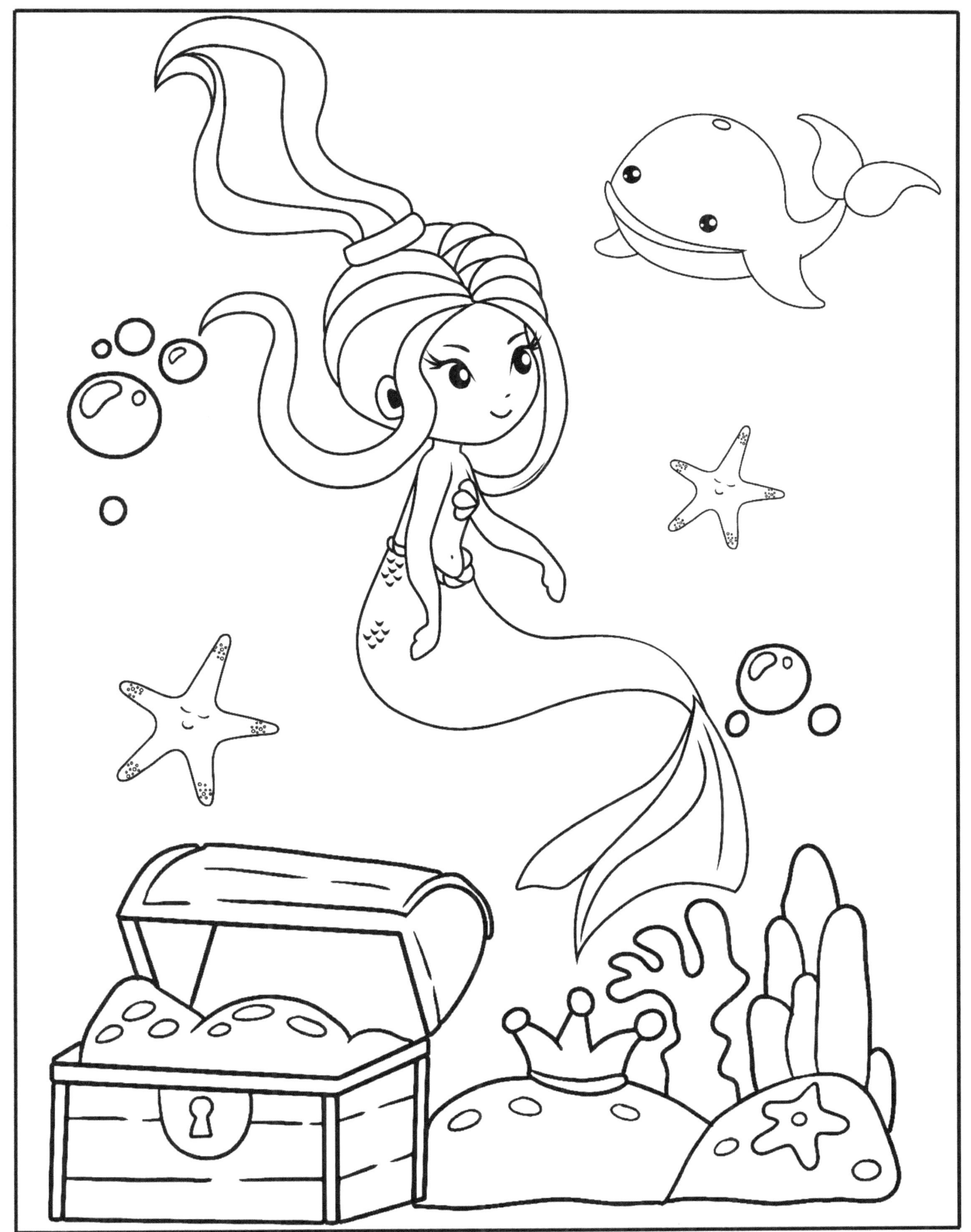

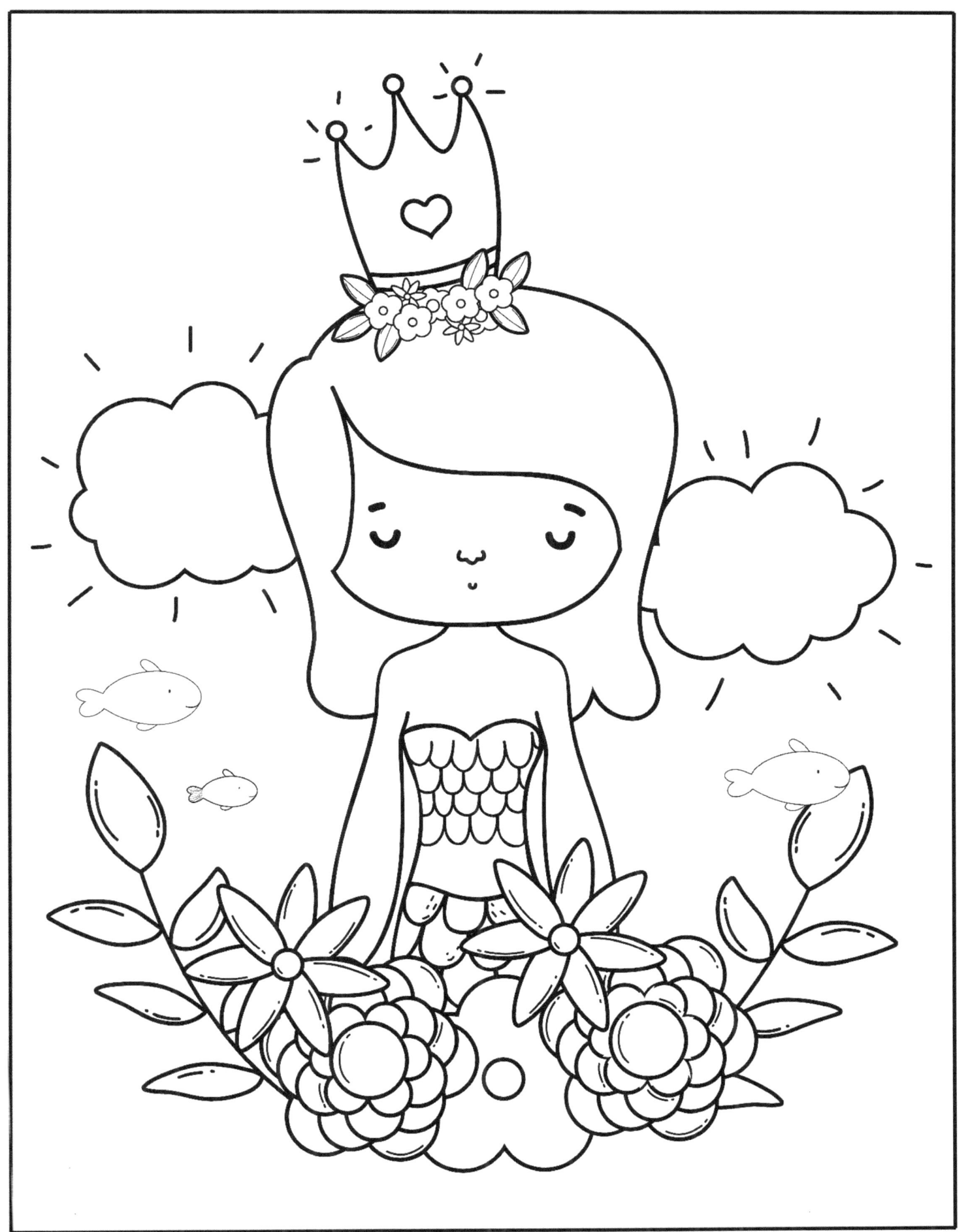

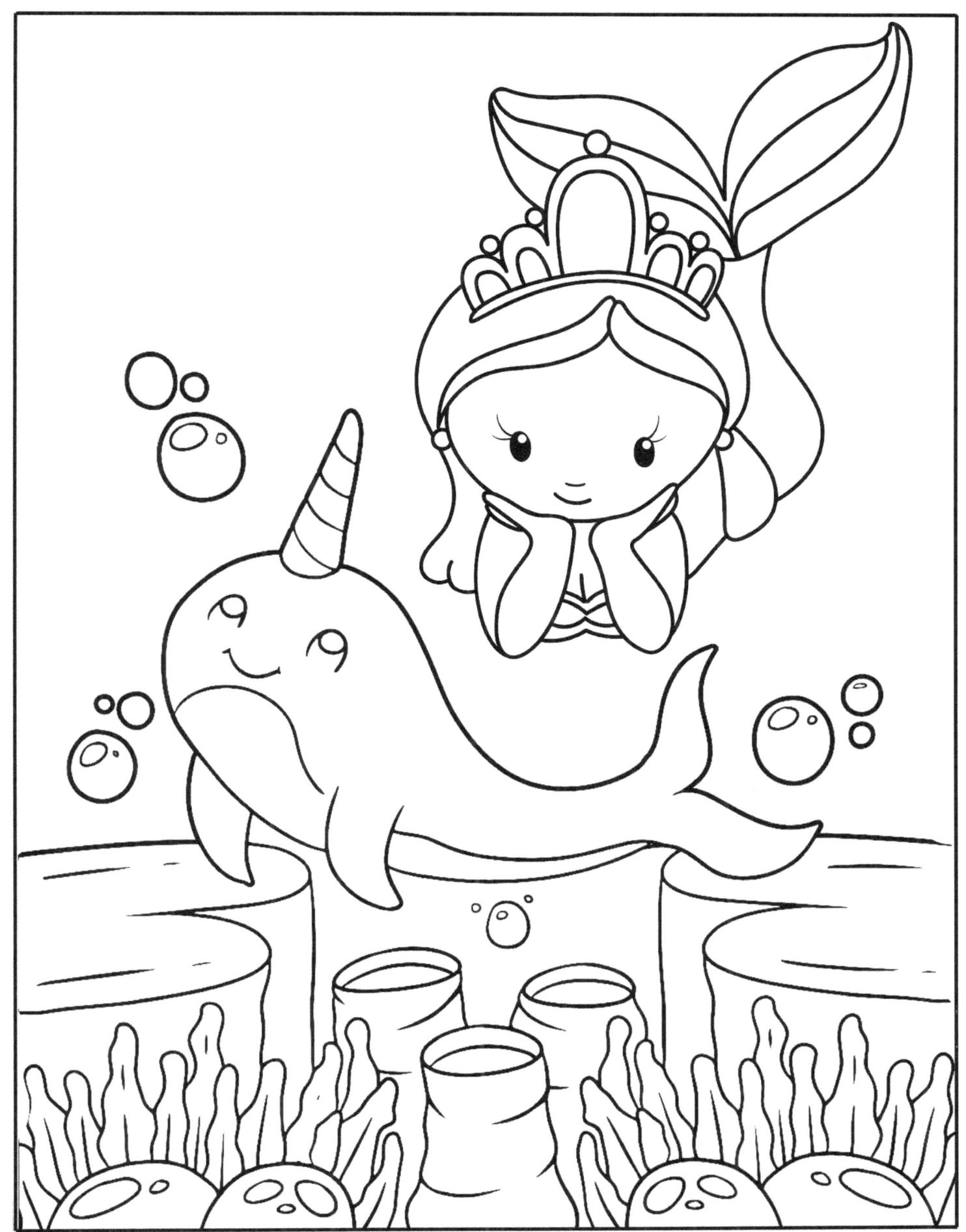

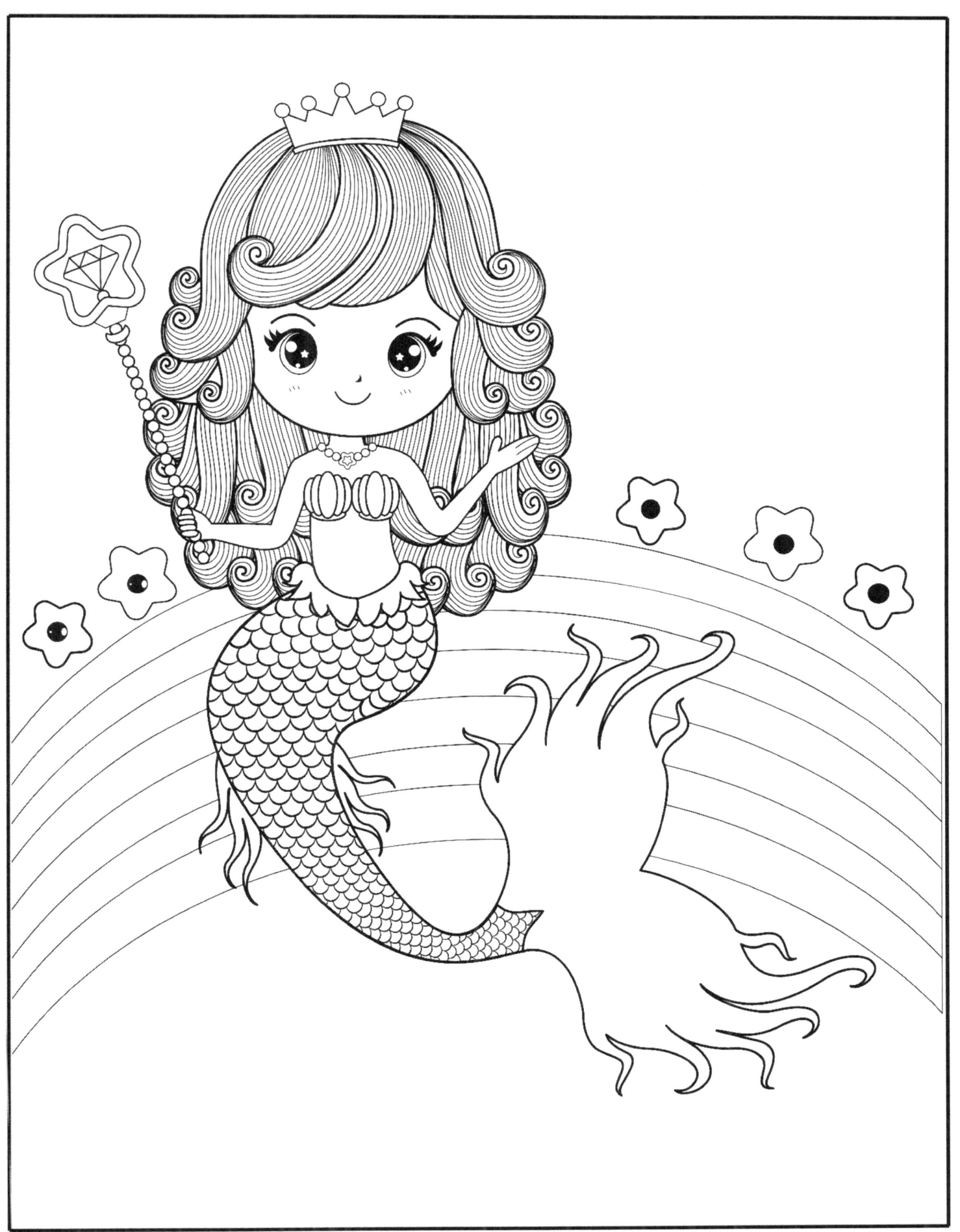

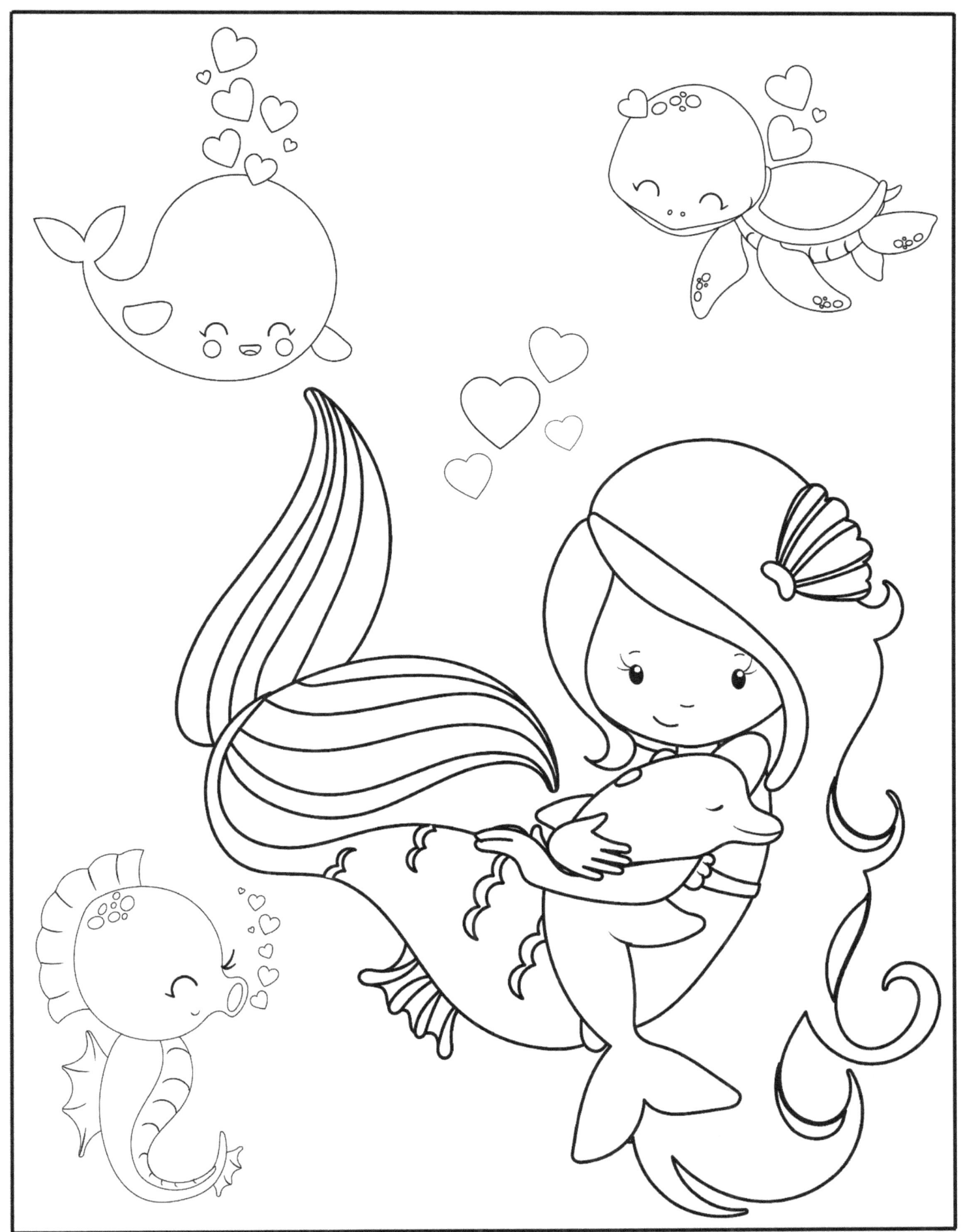

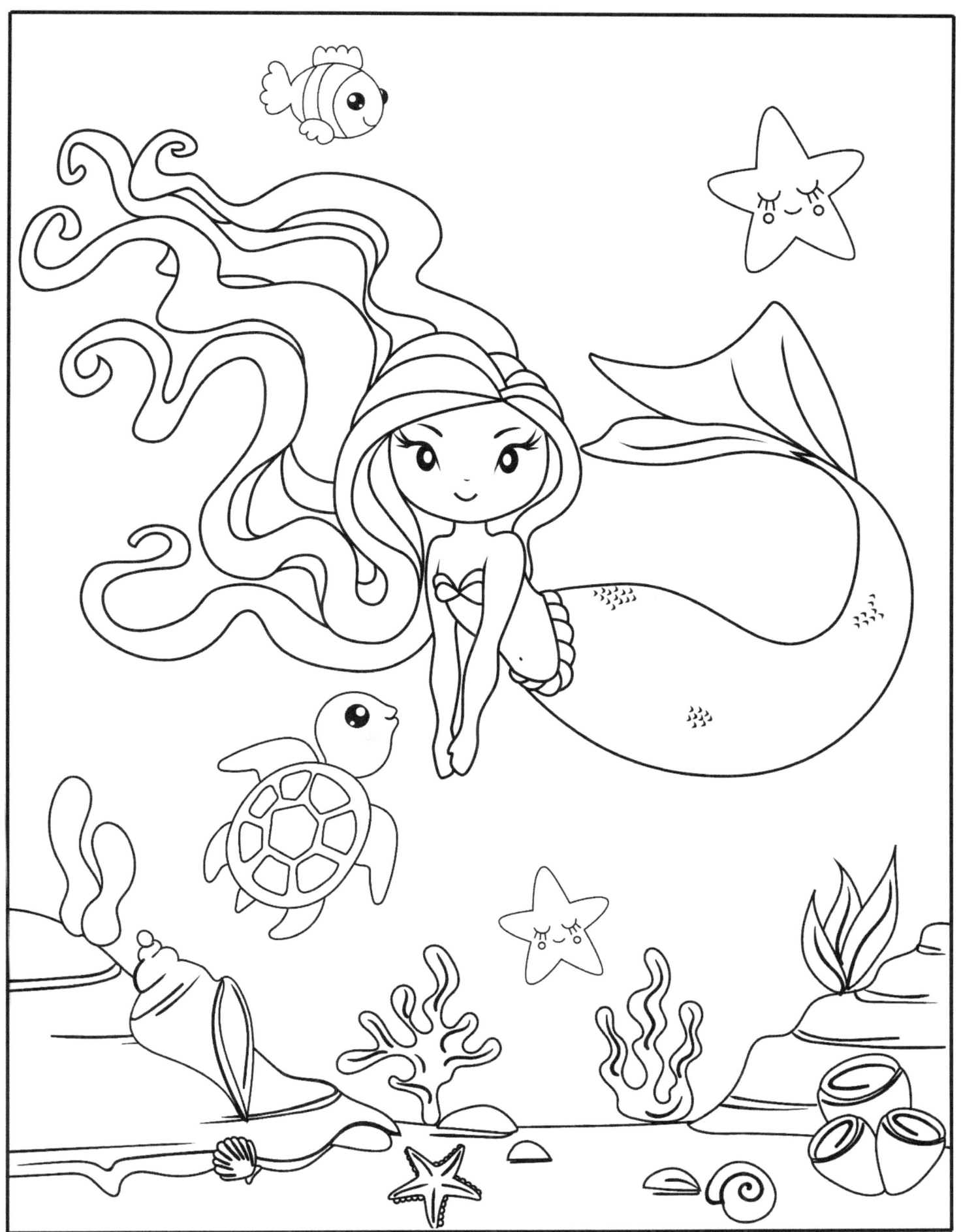

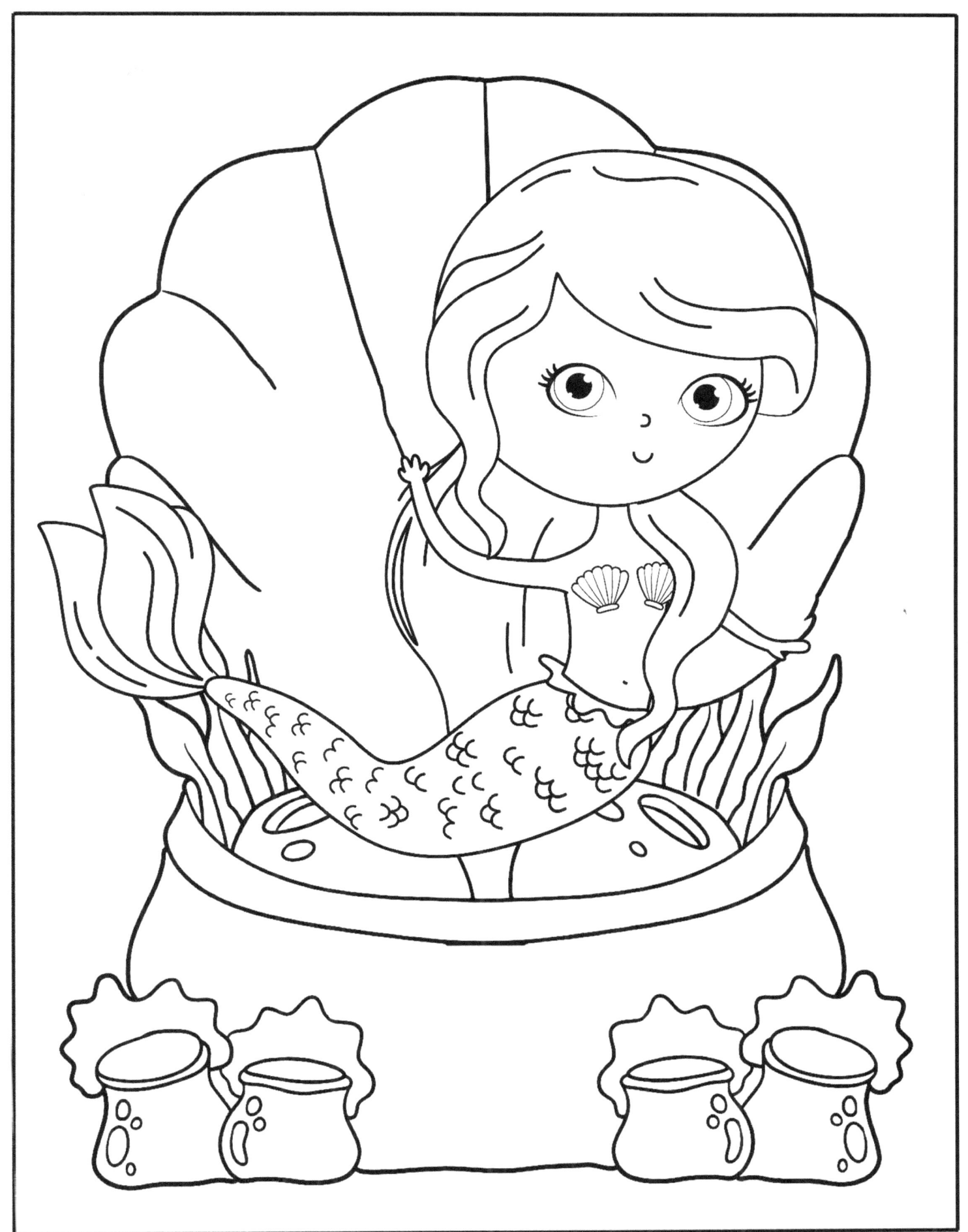

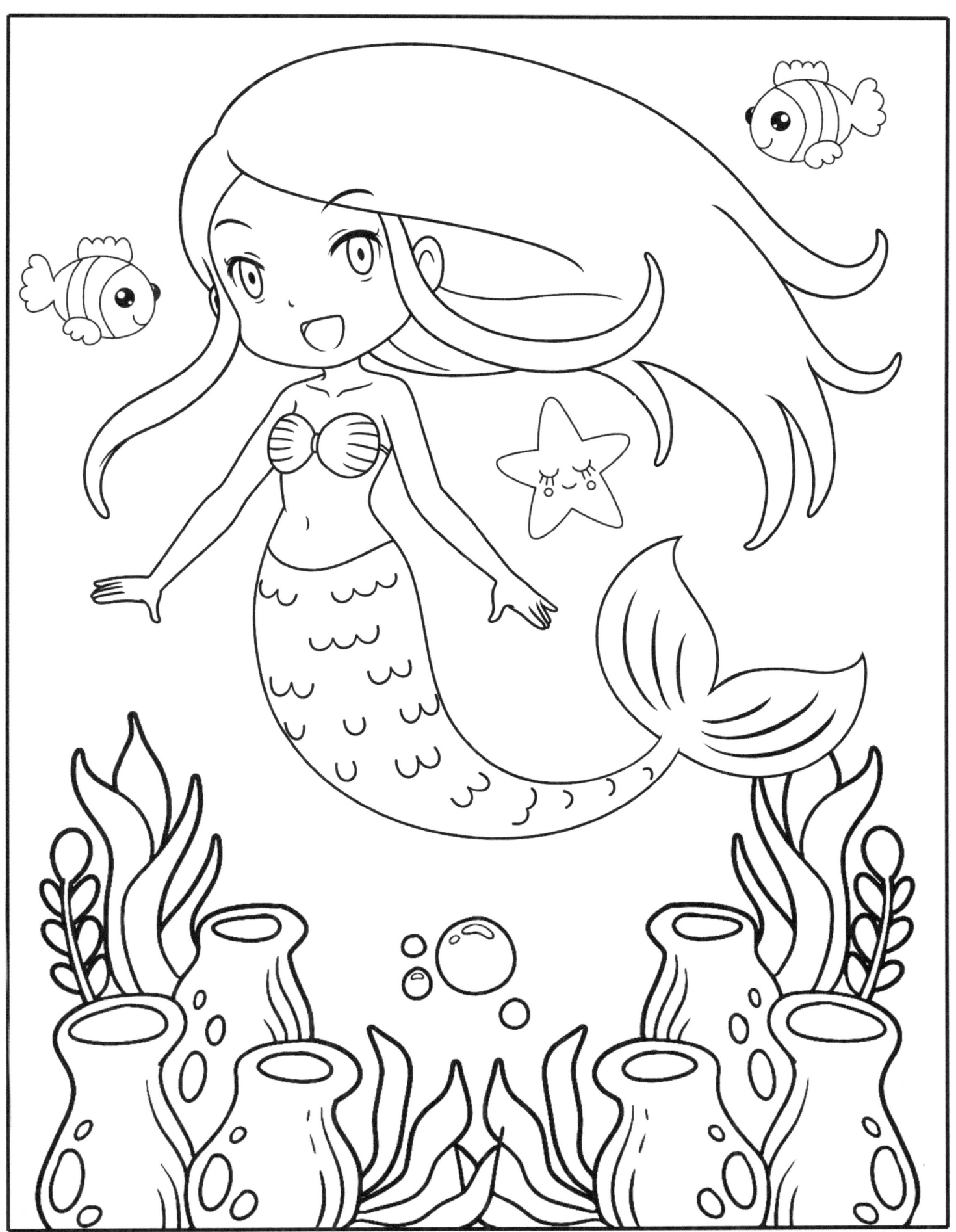

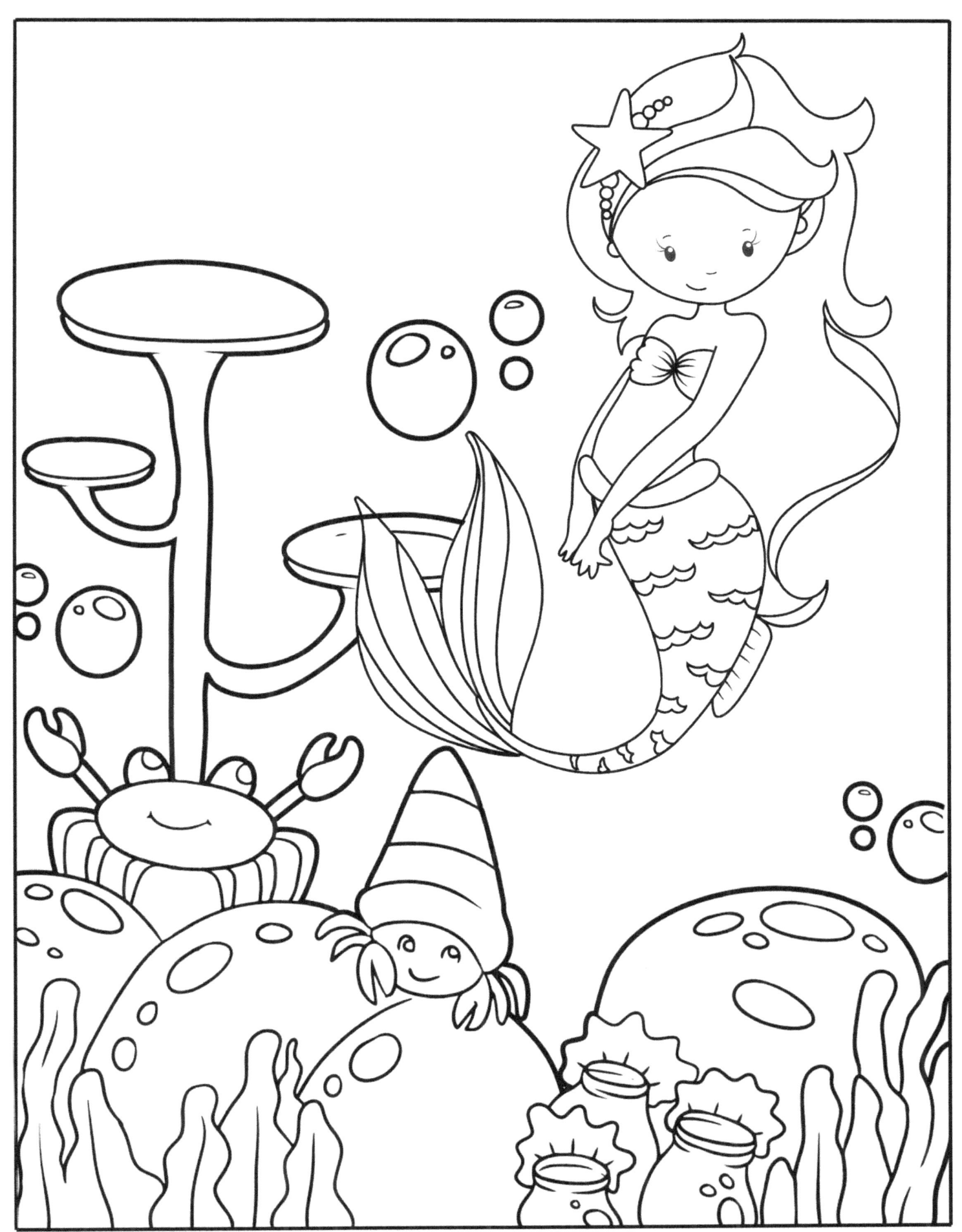

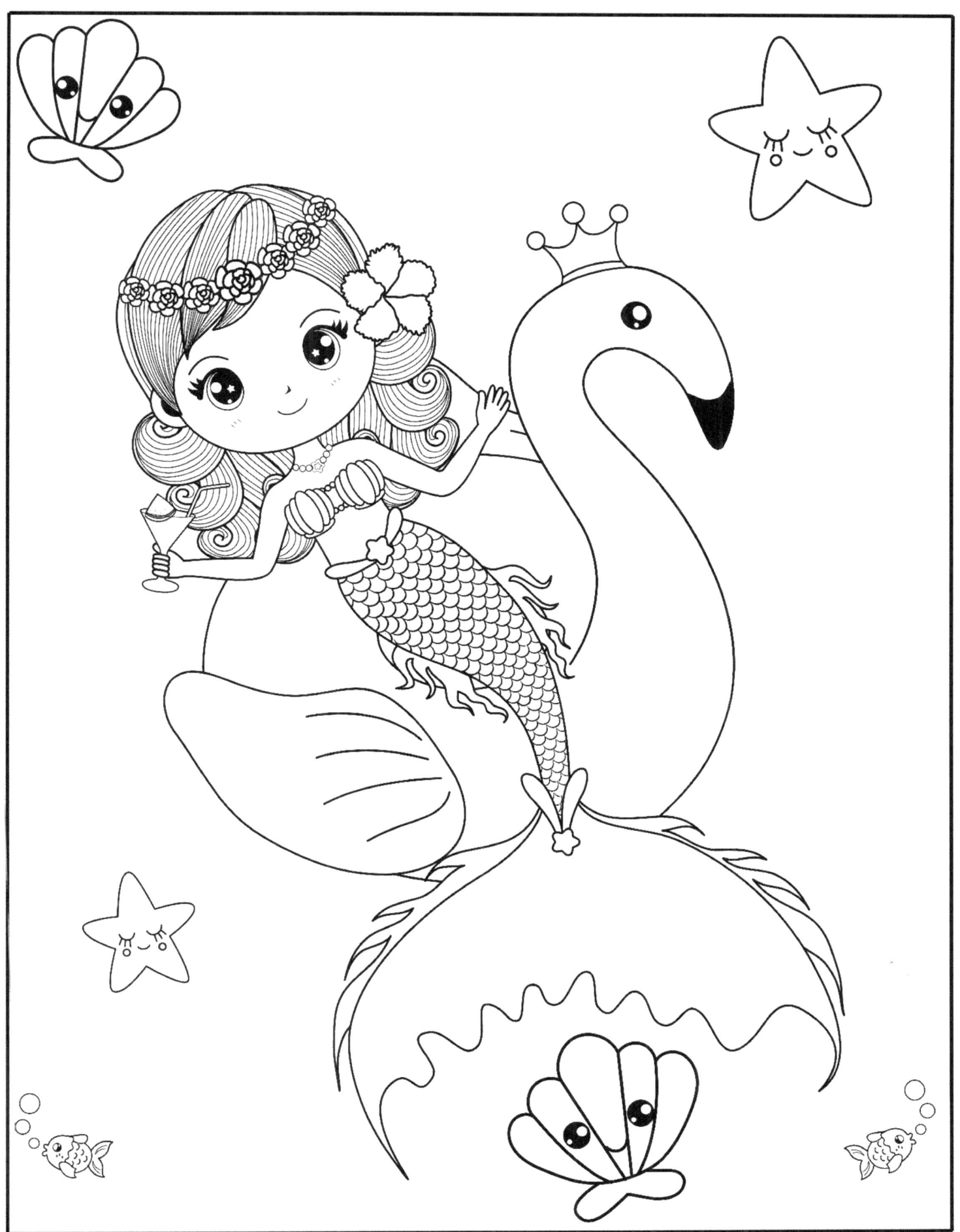

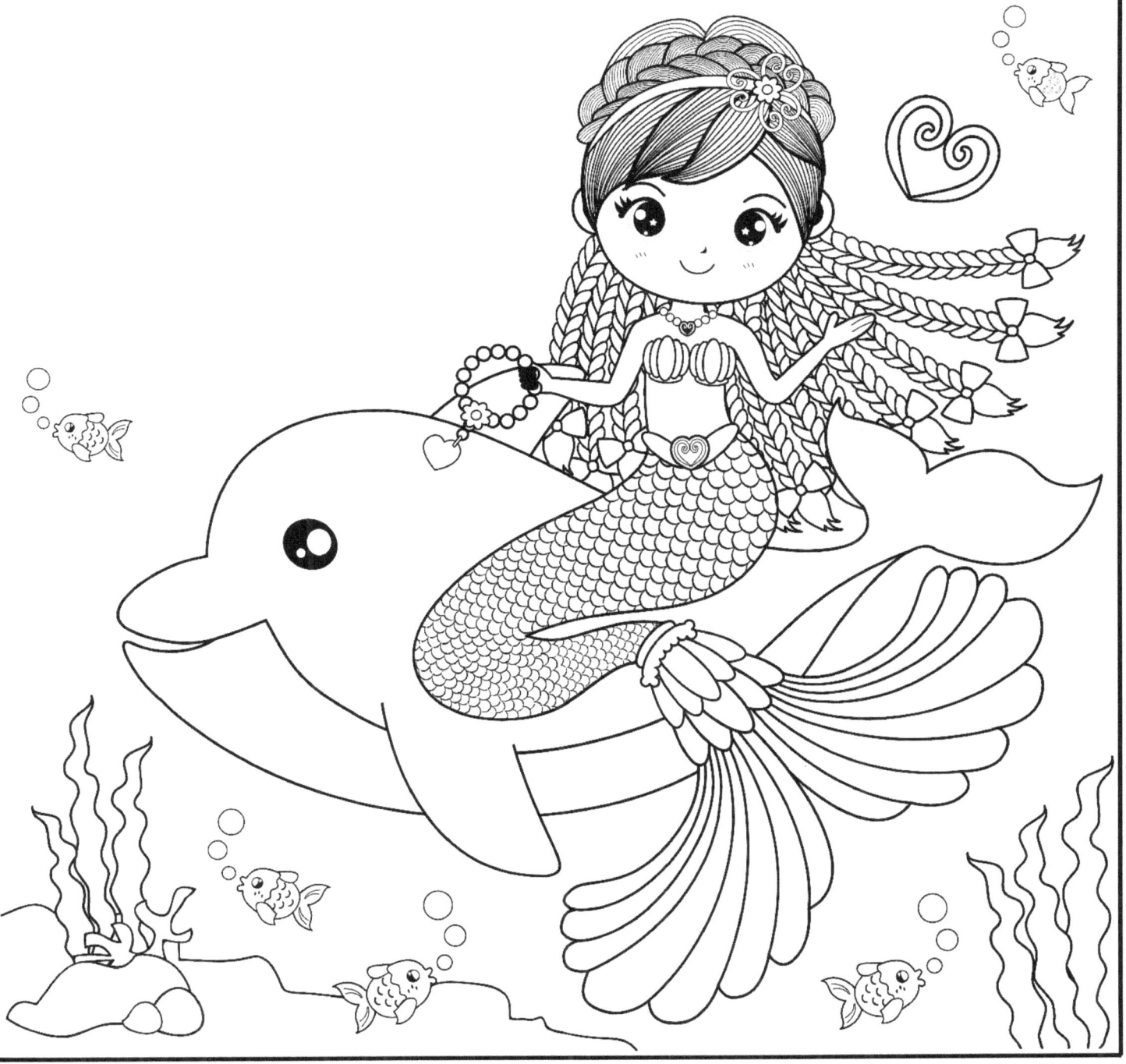

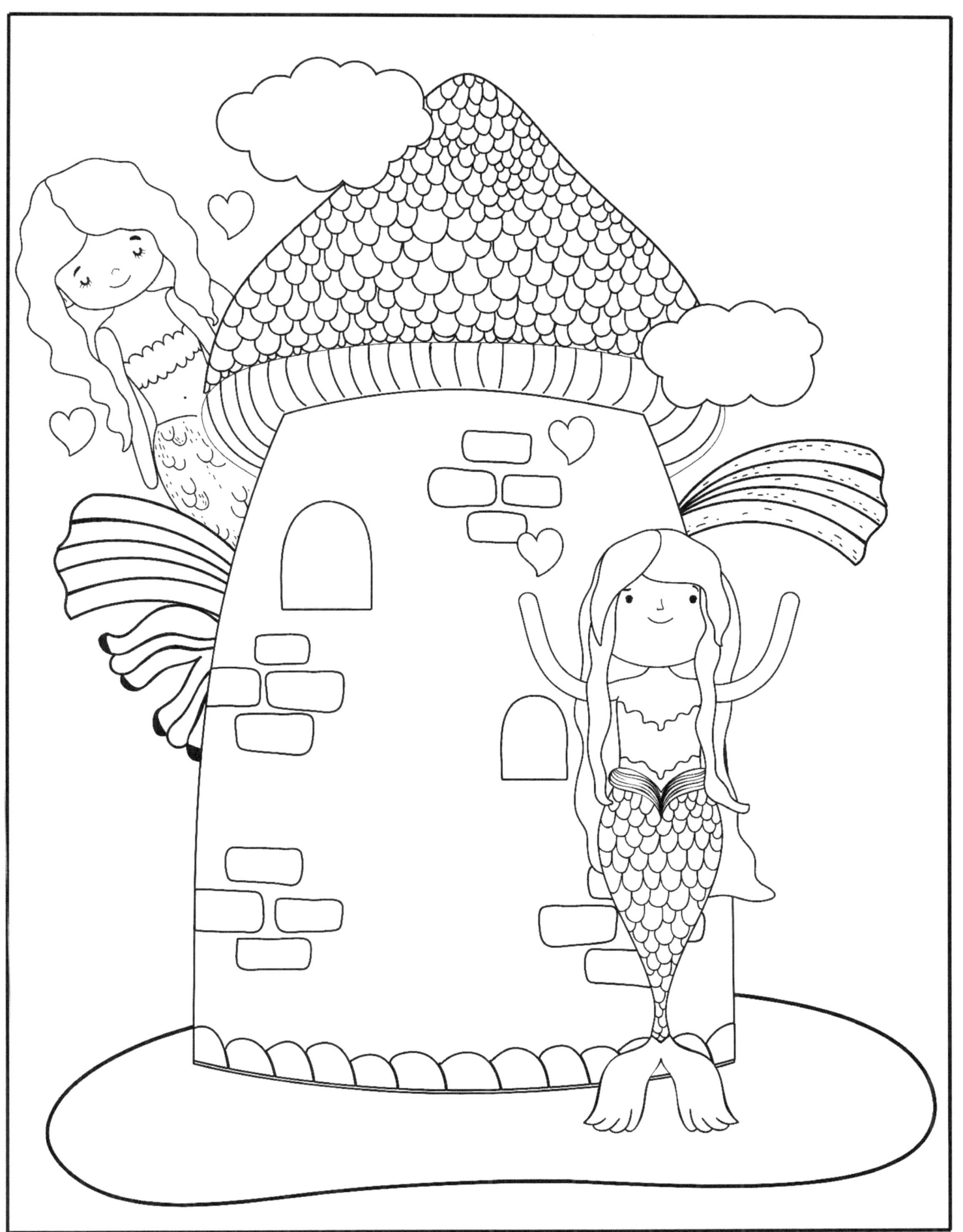

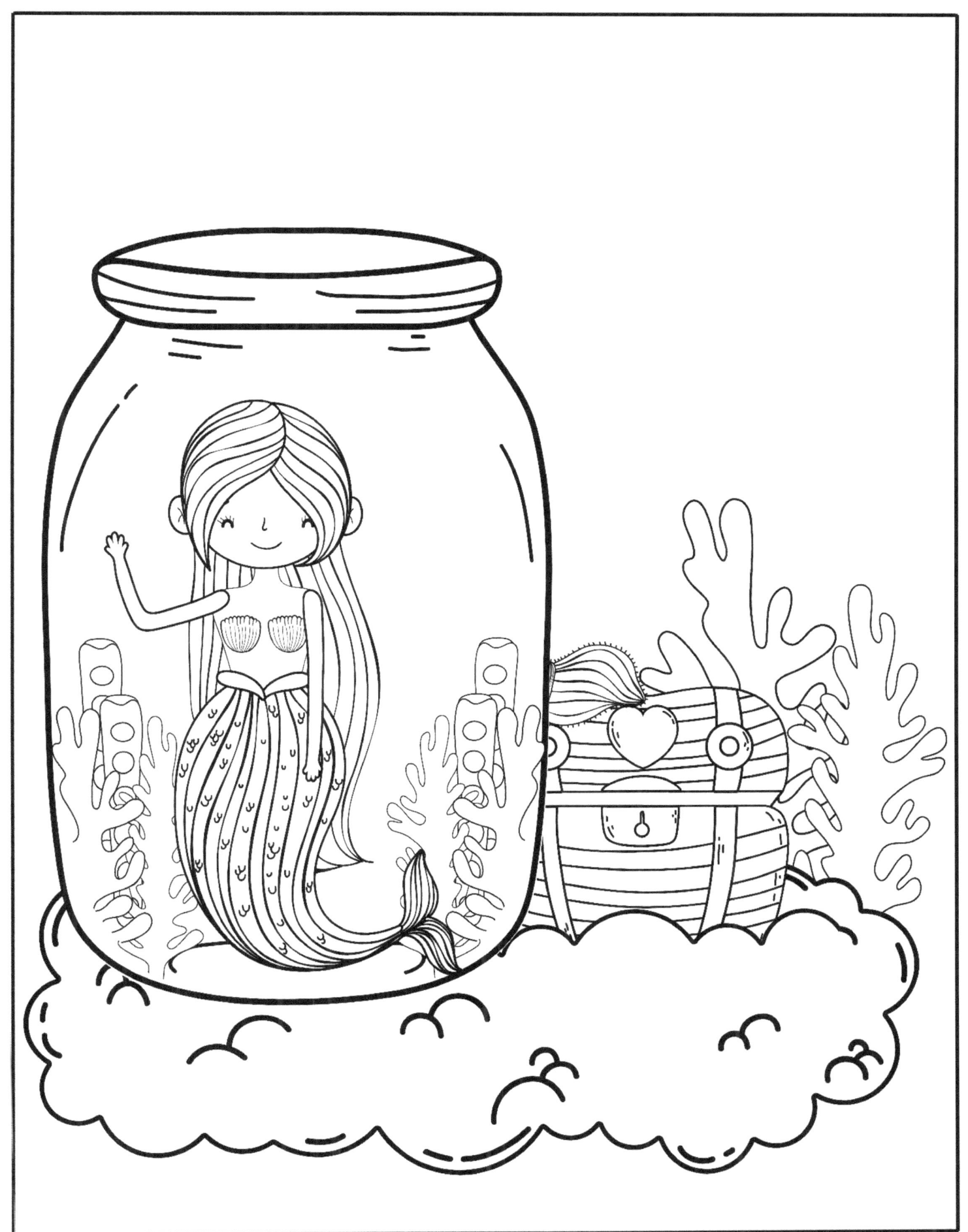

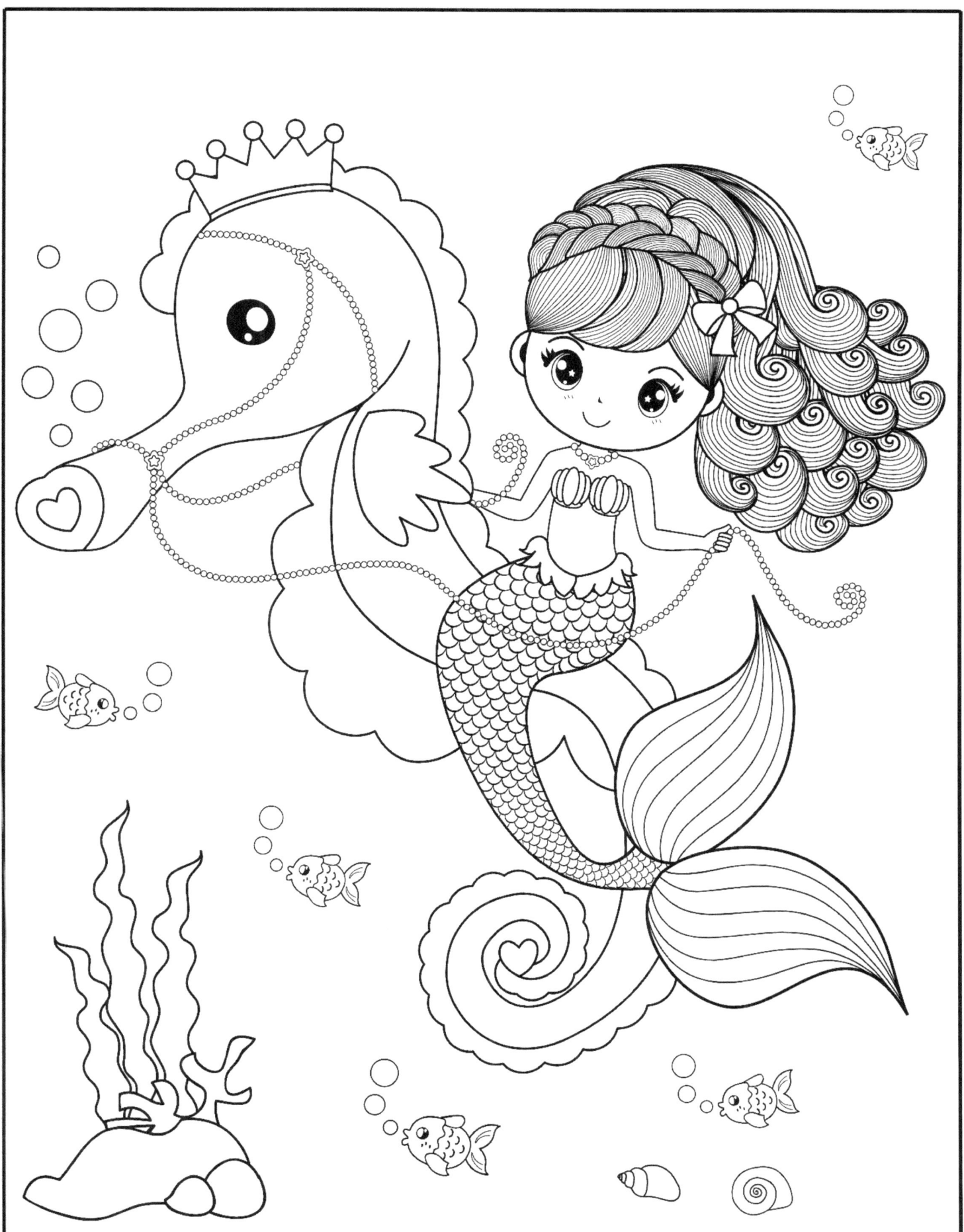

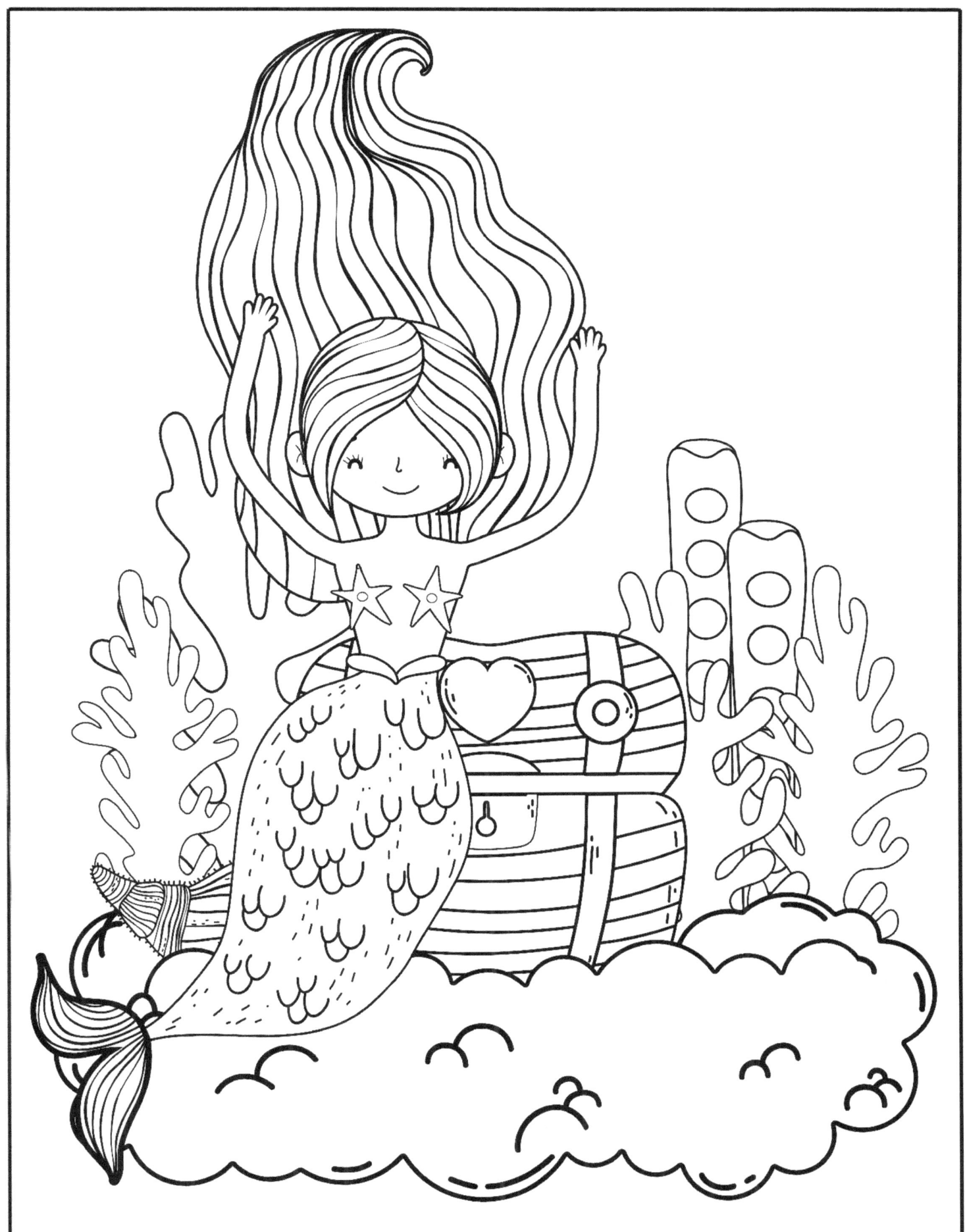

MERMAID

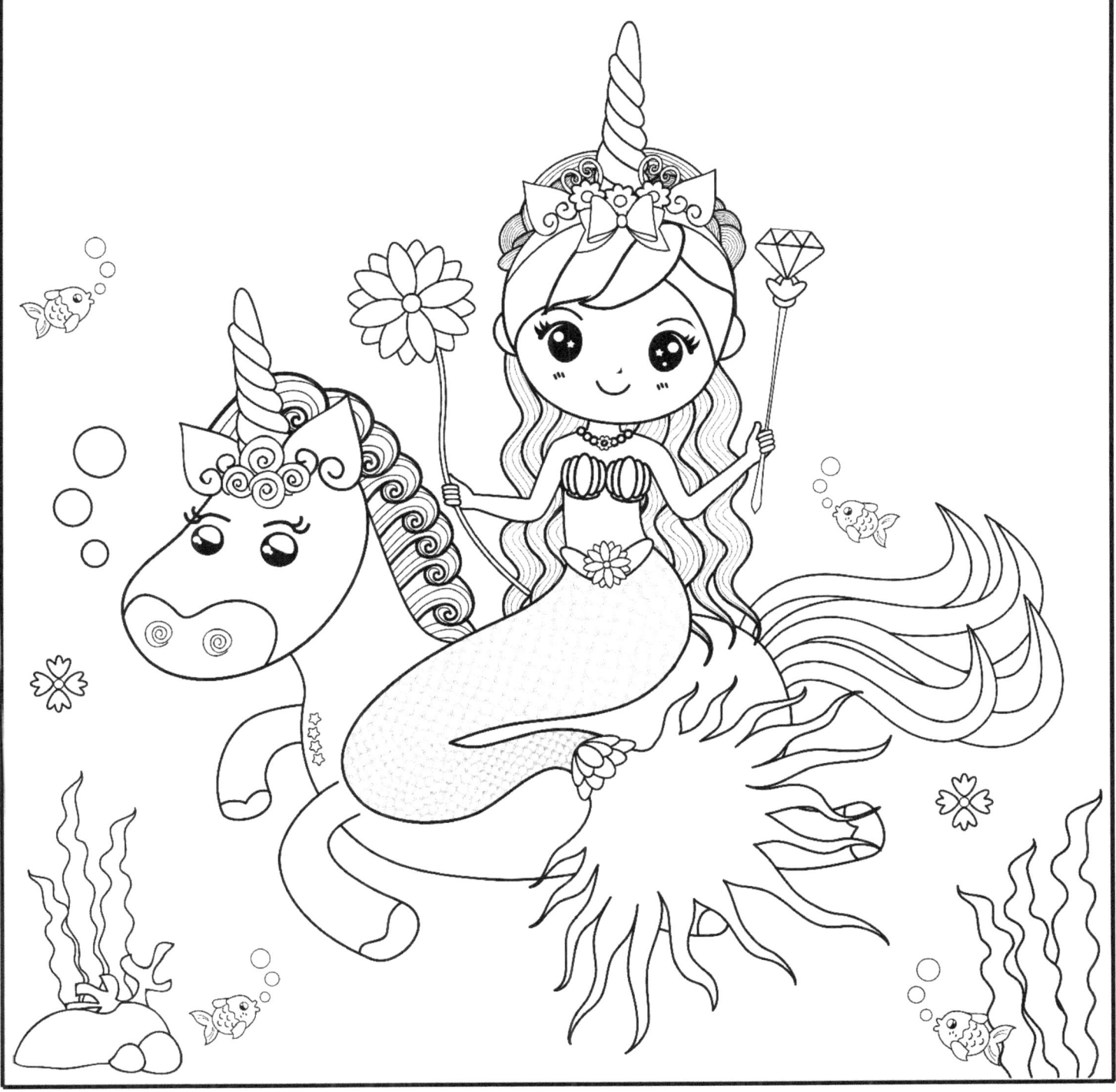

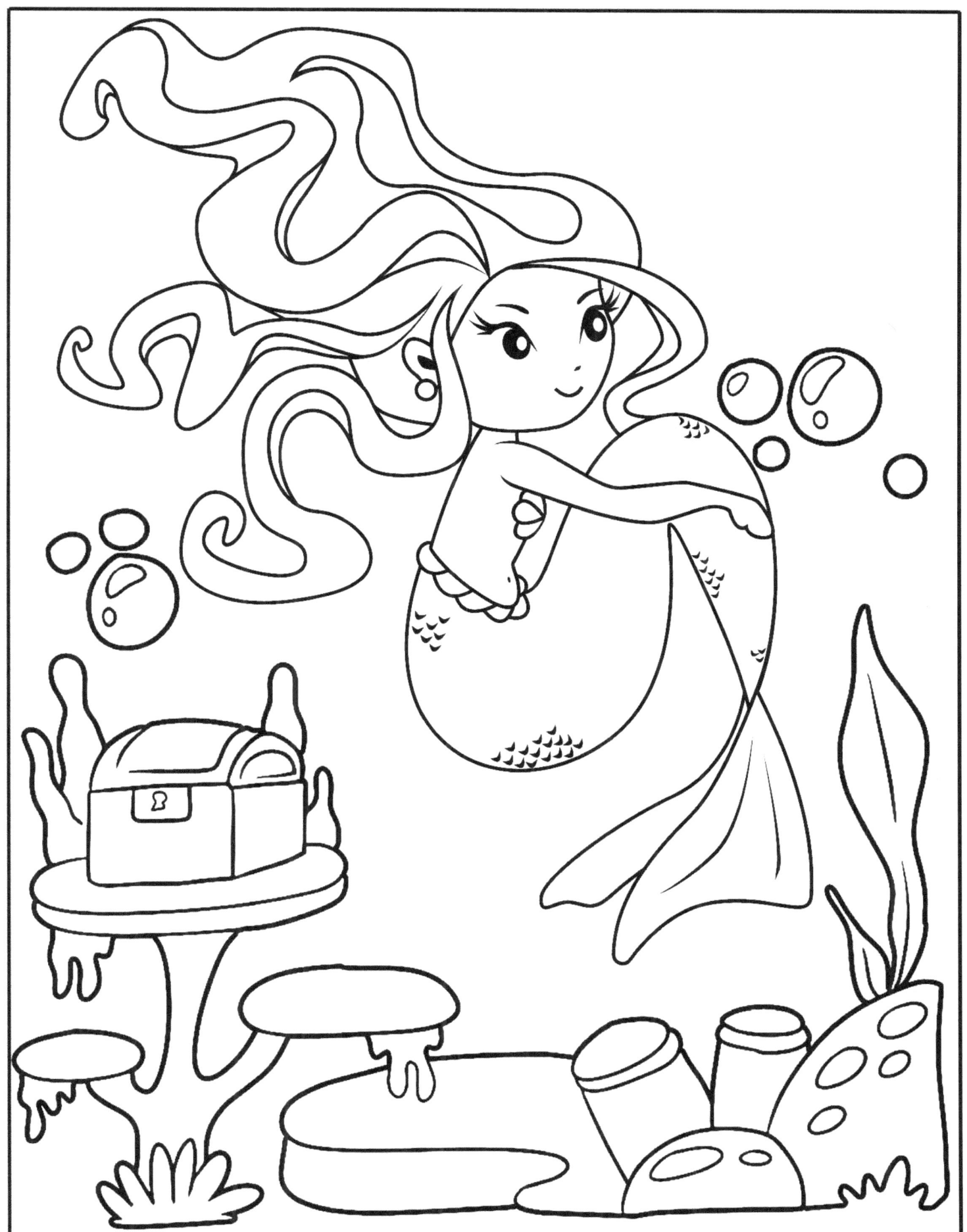

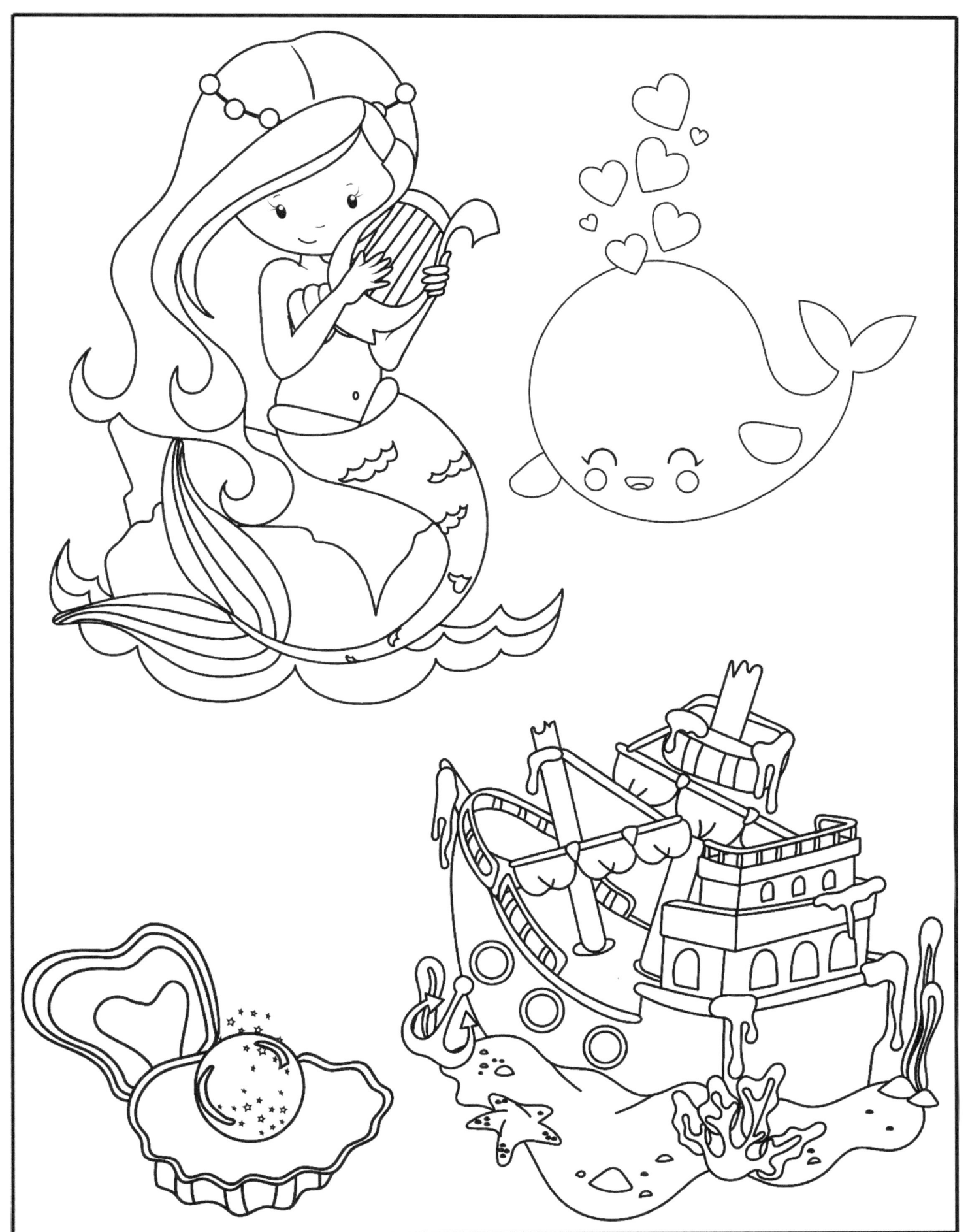

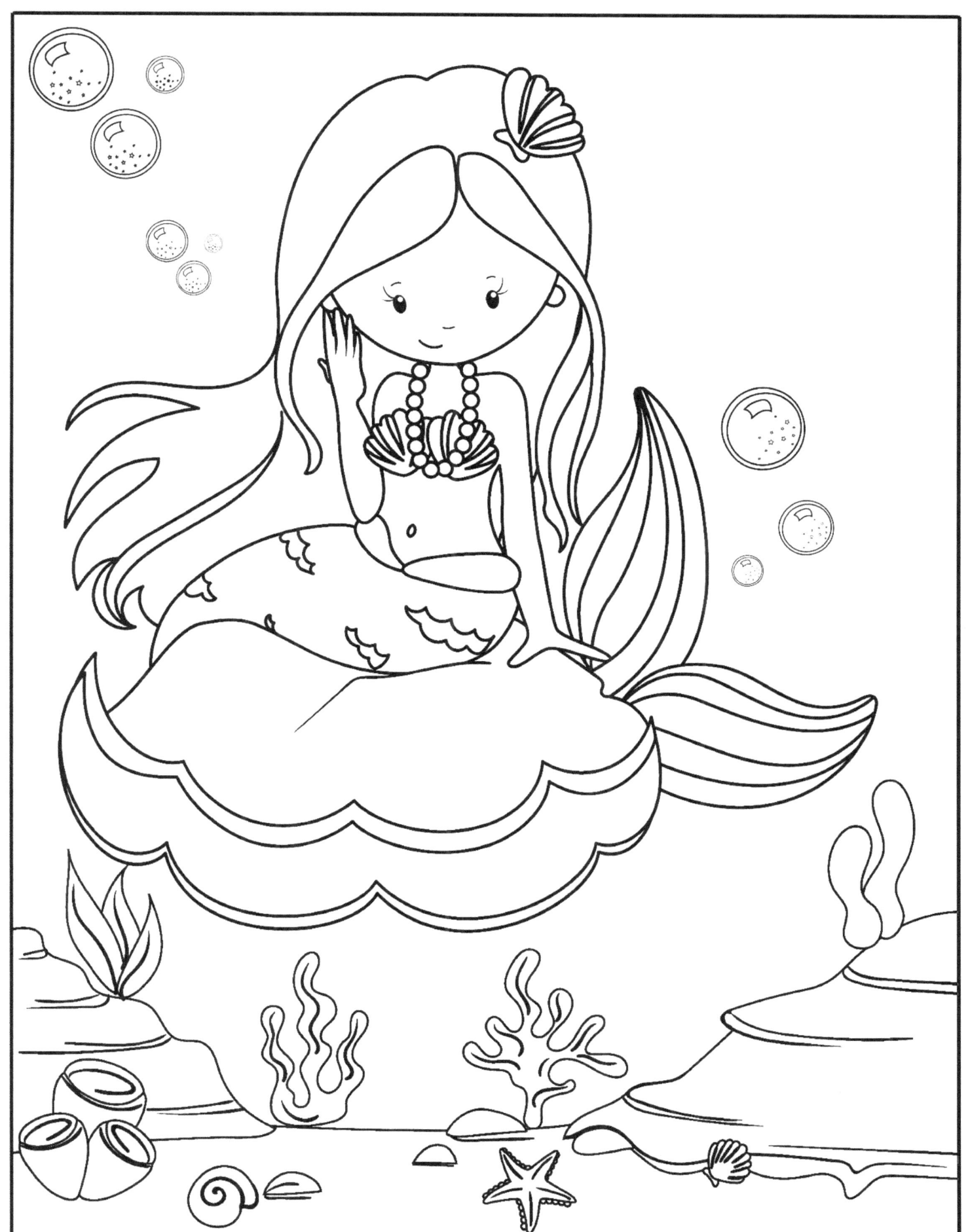

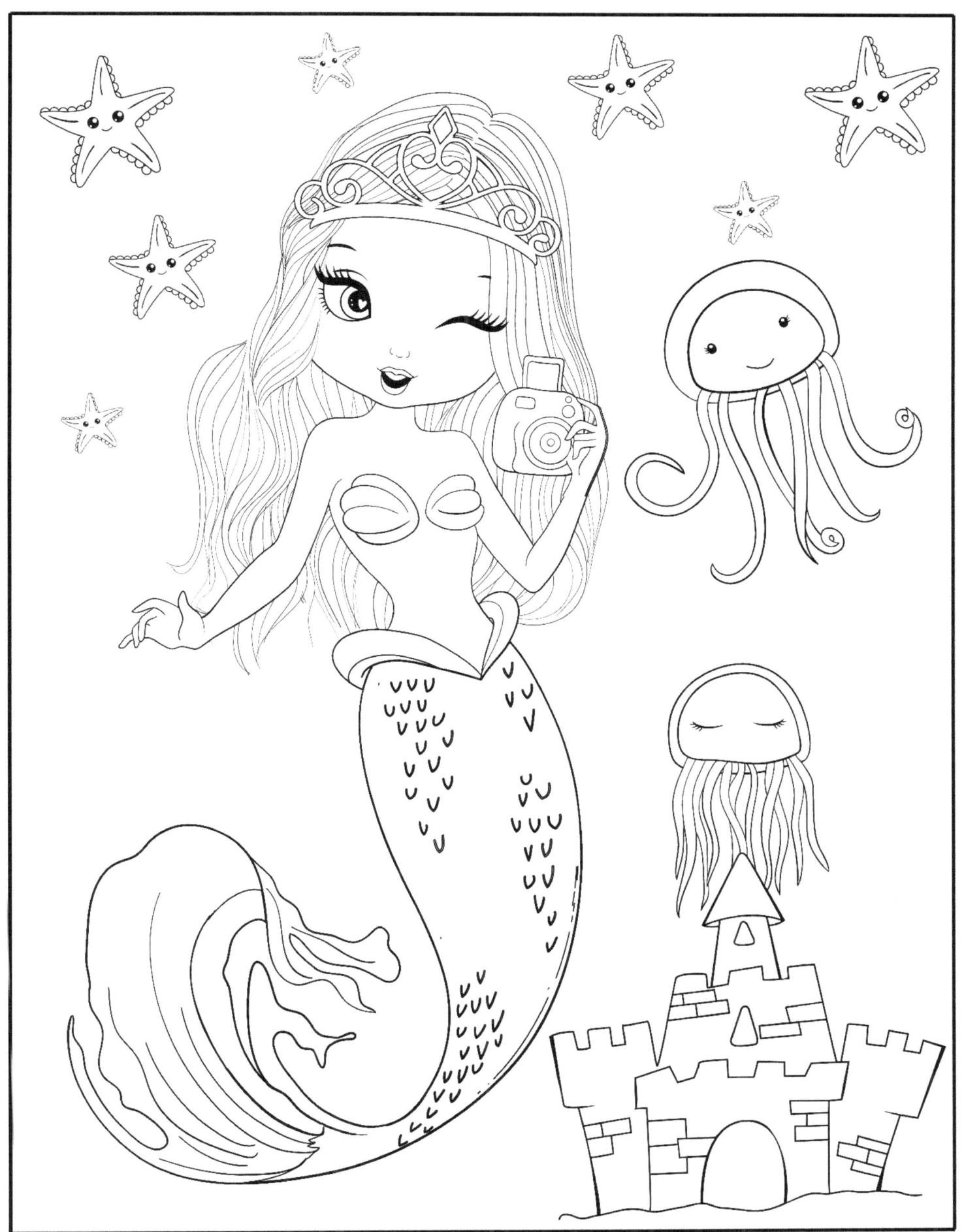

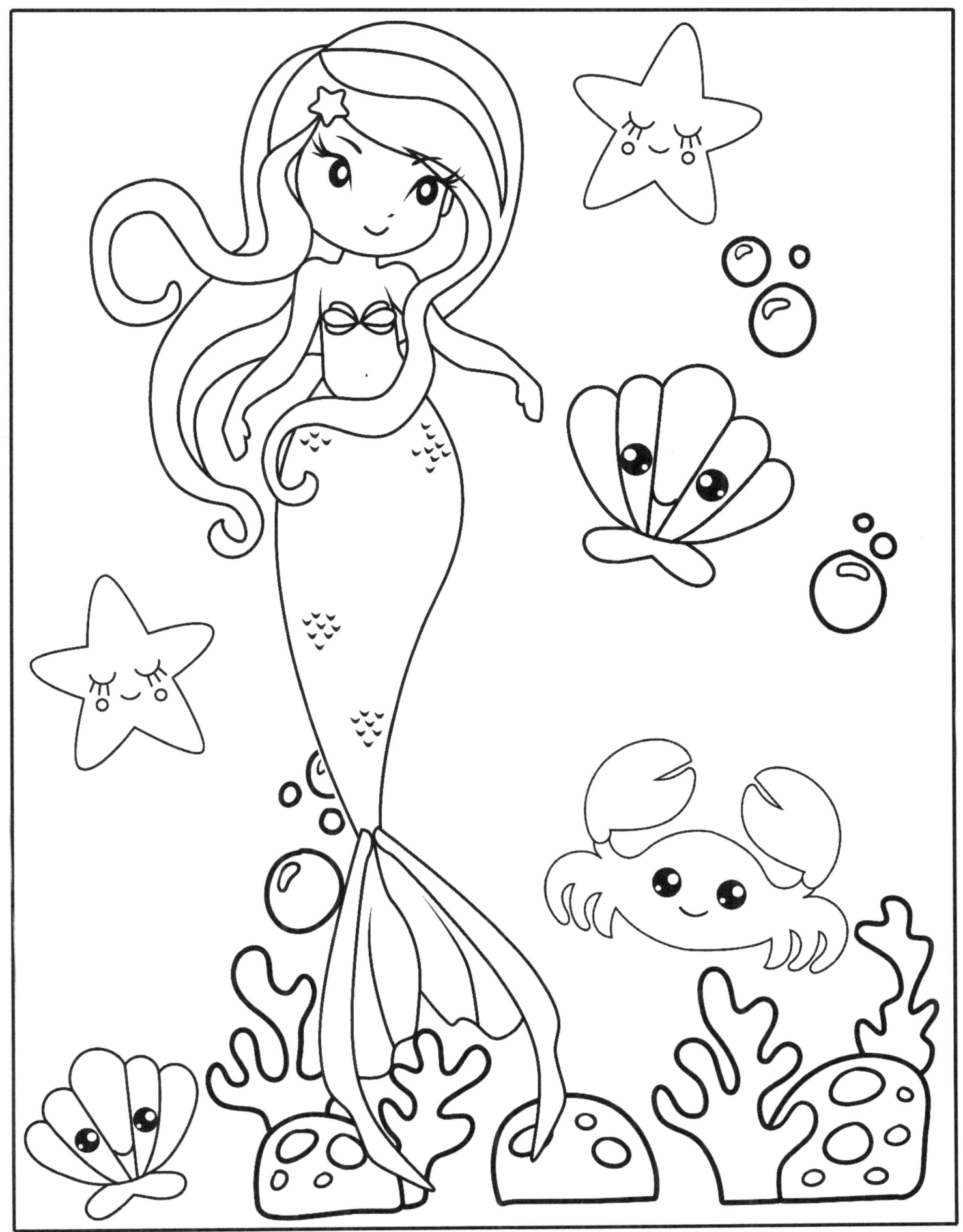

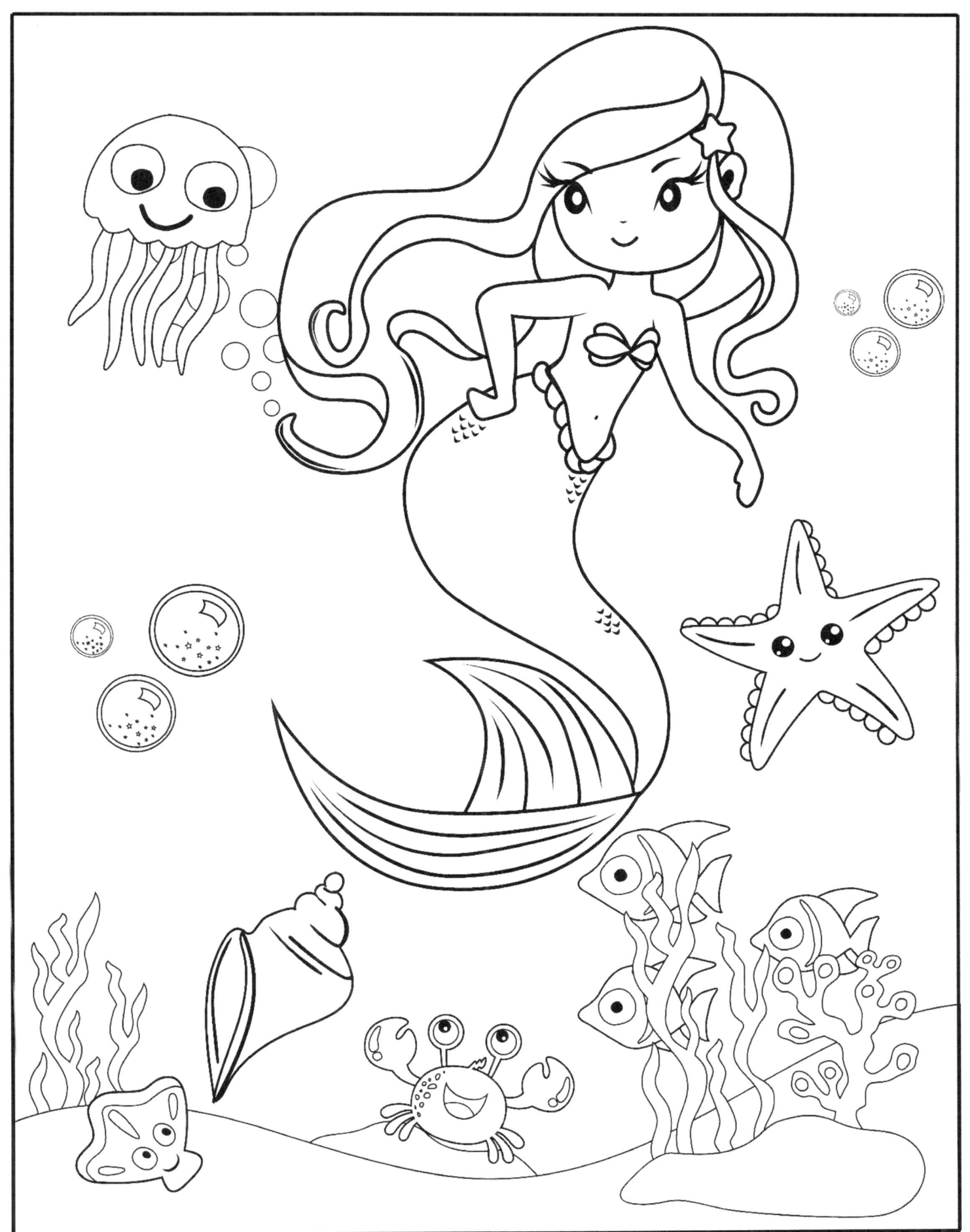

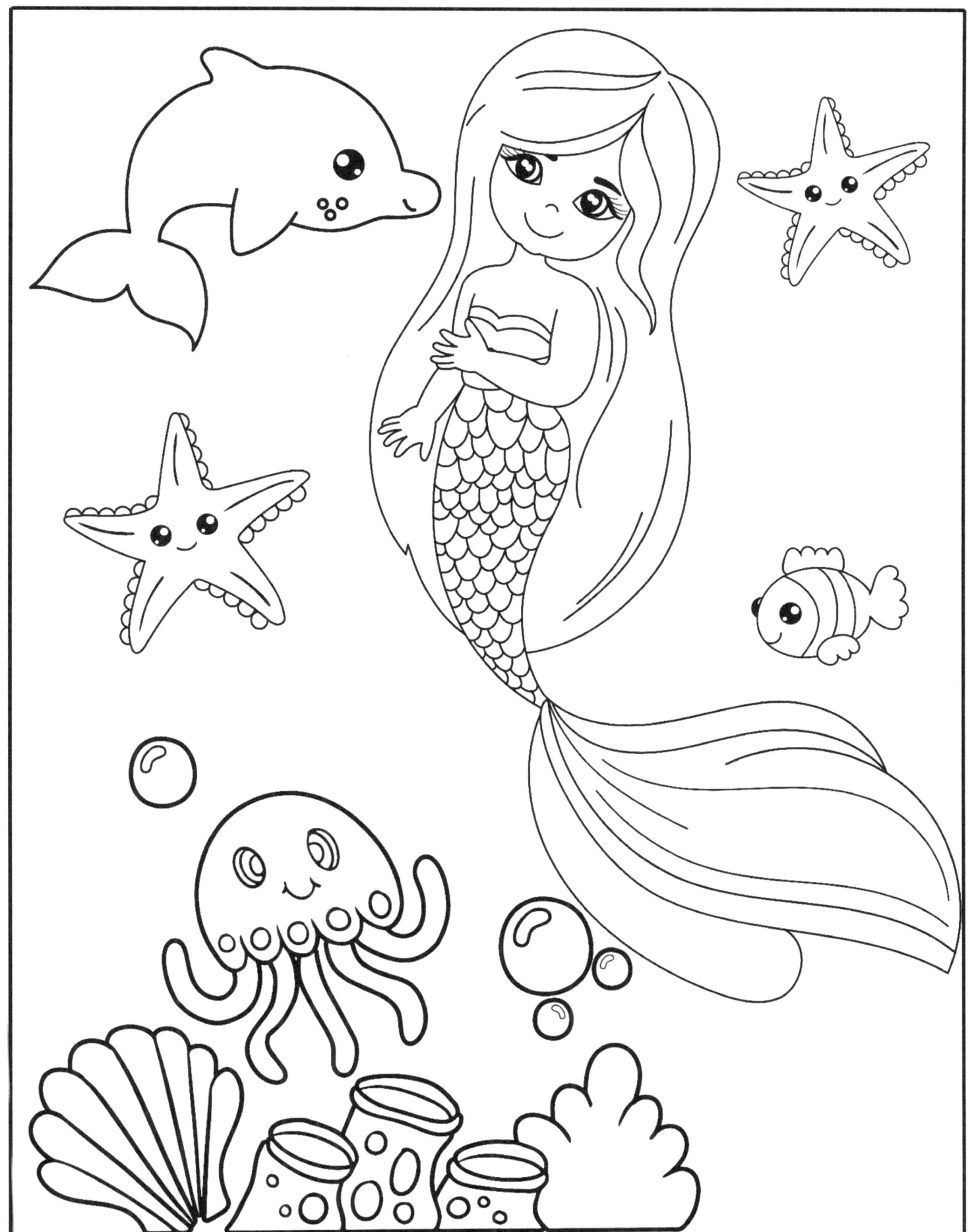

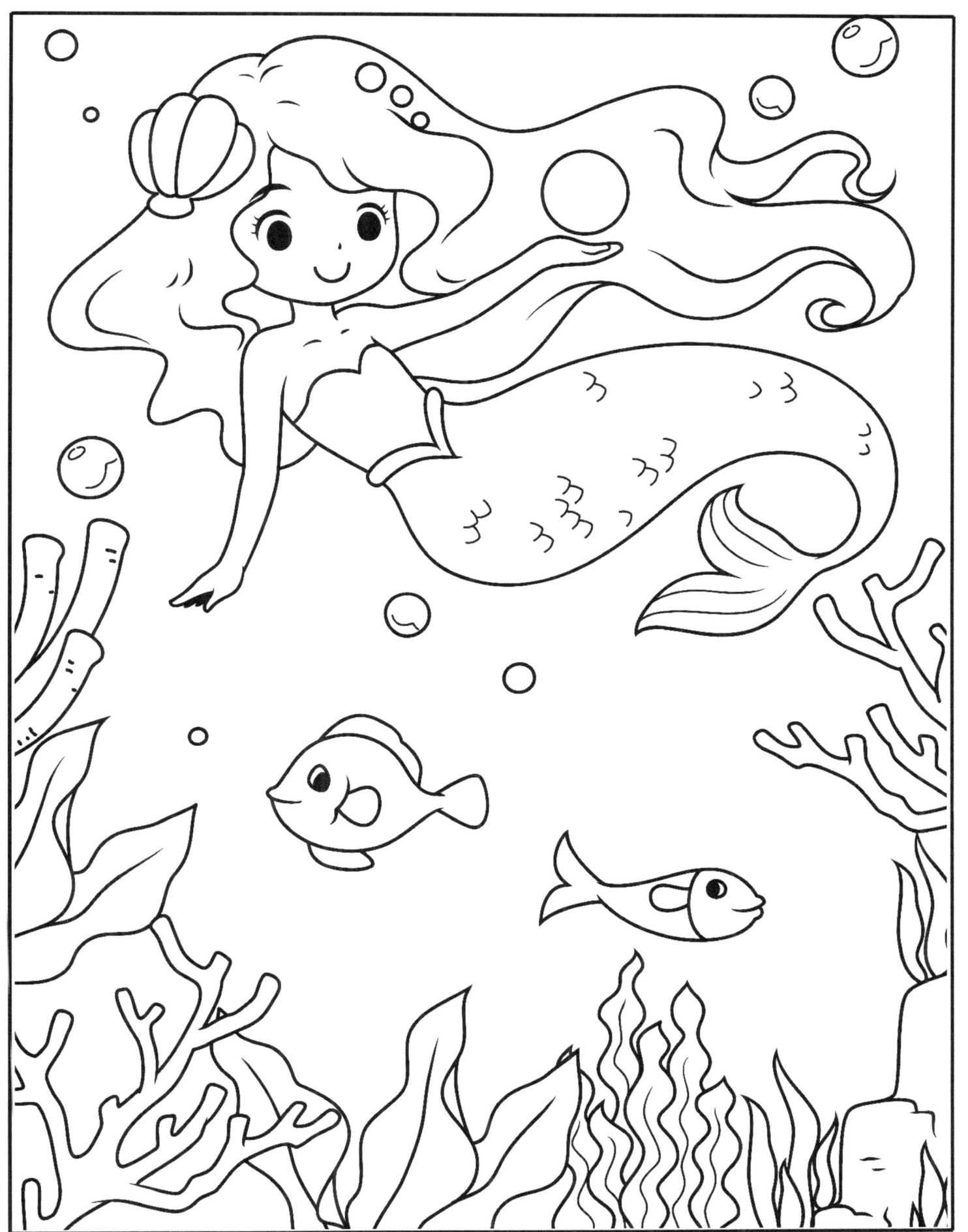

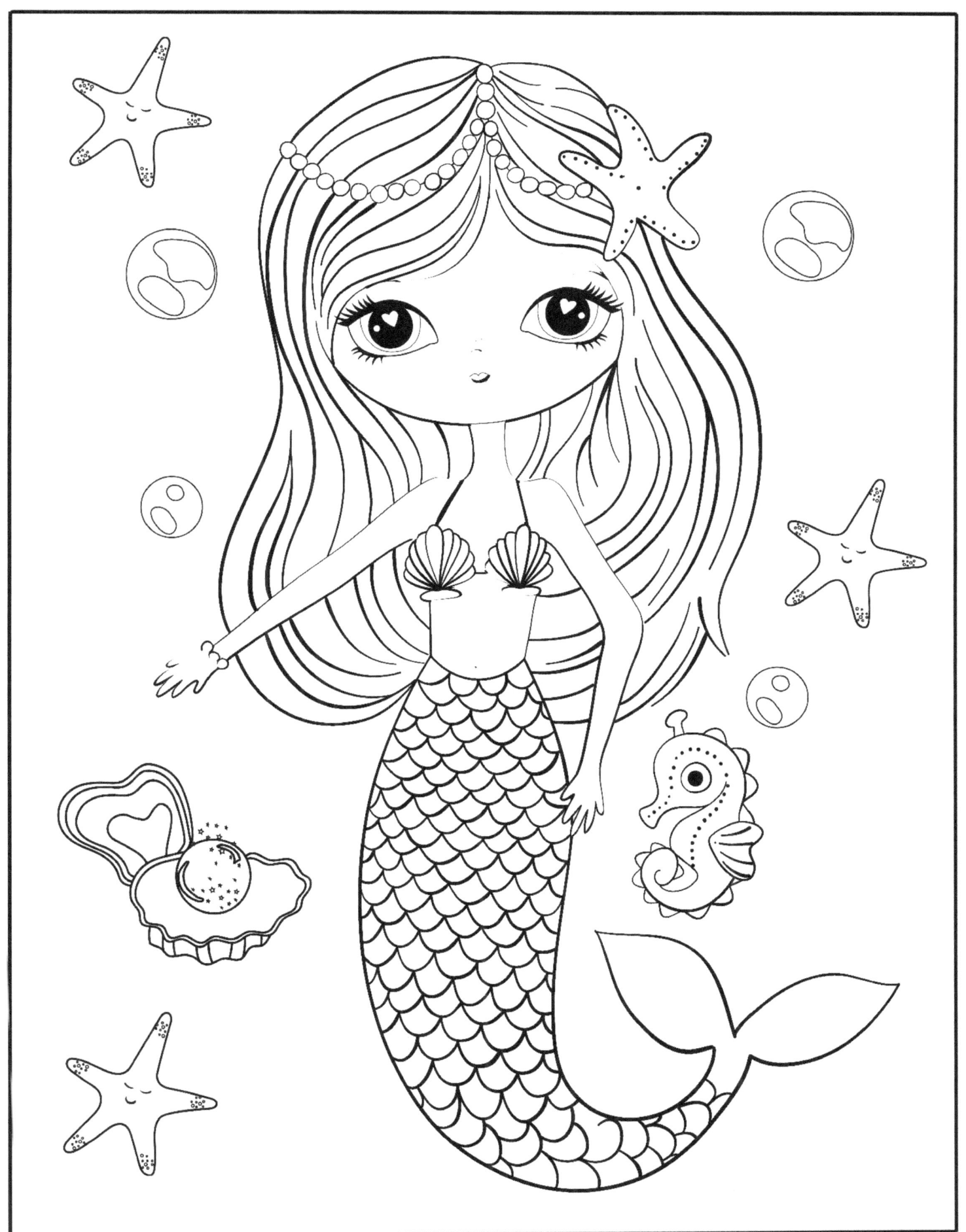

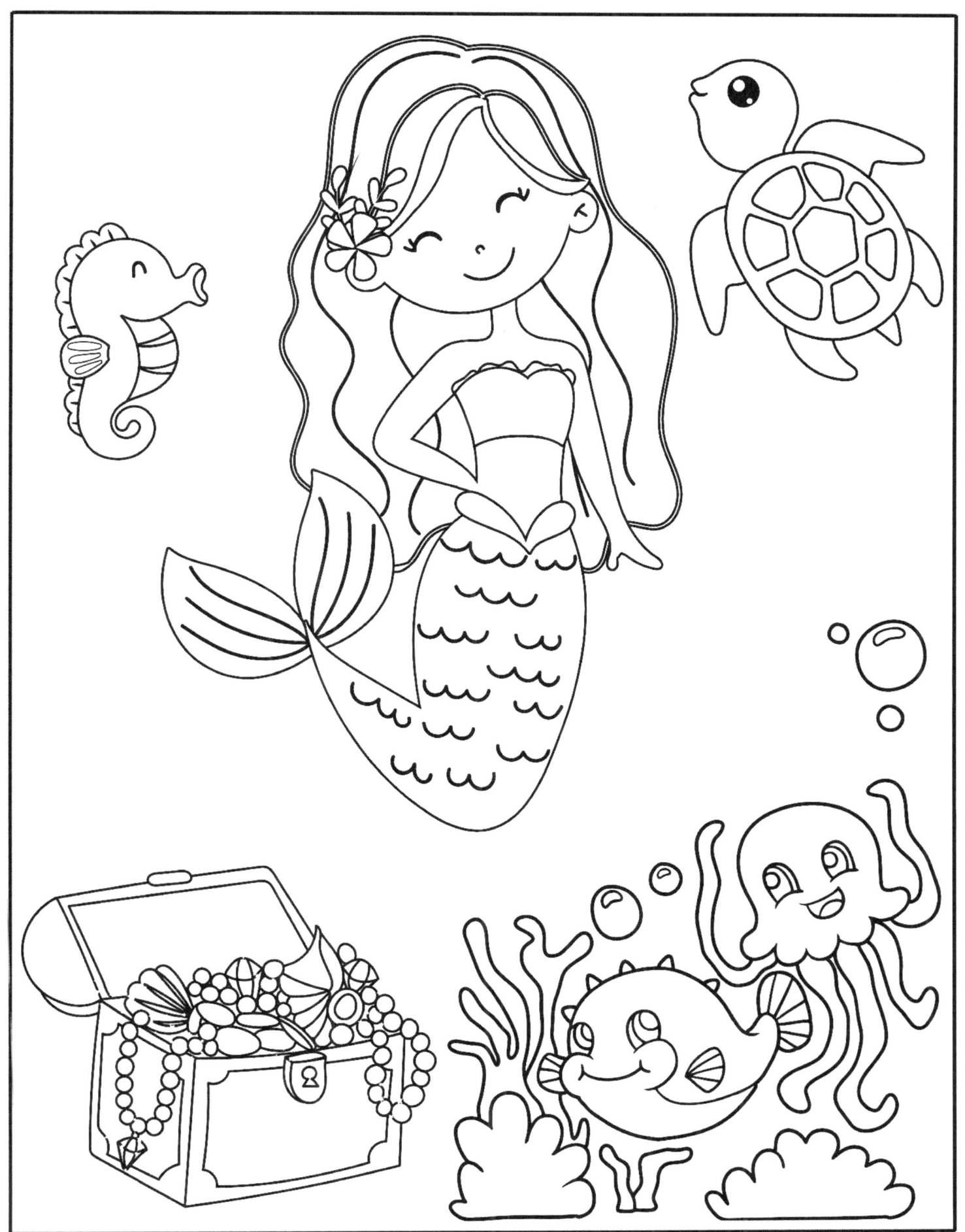

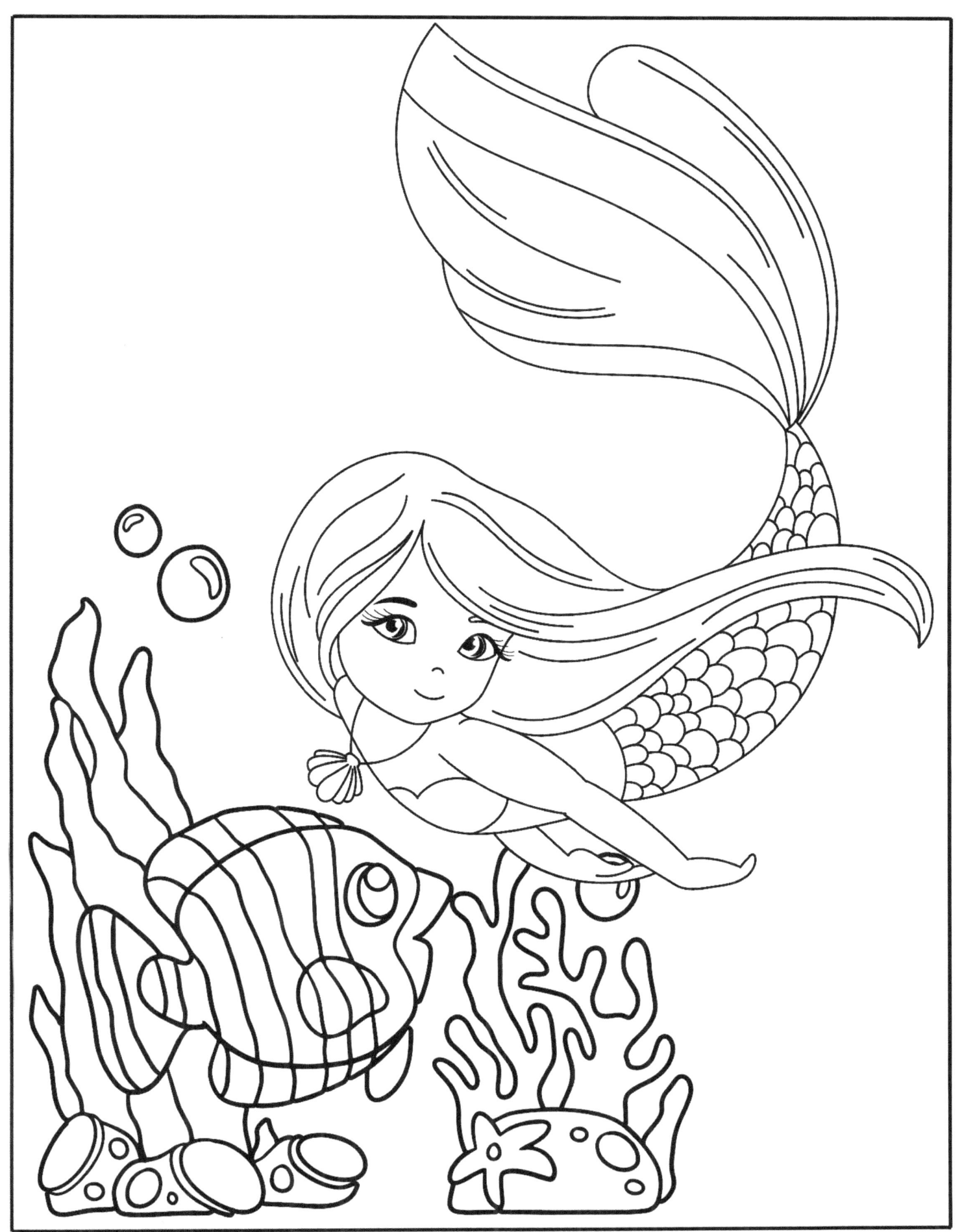

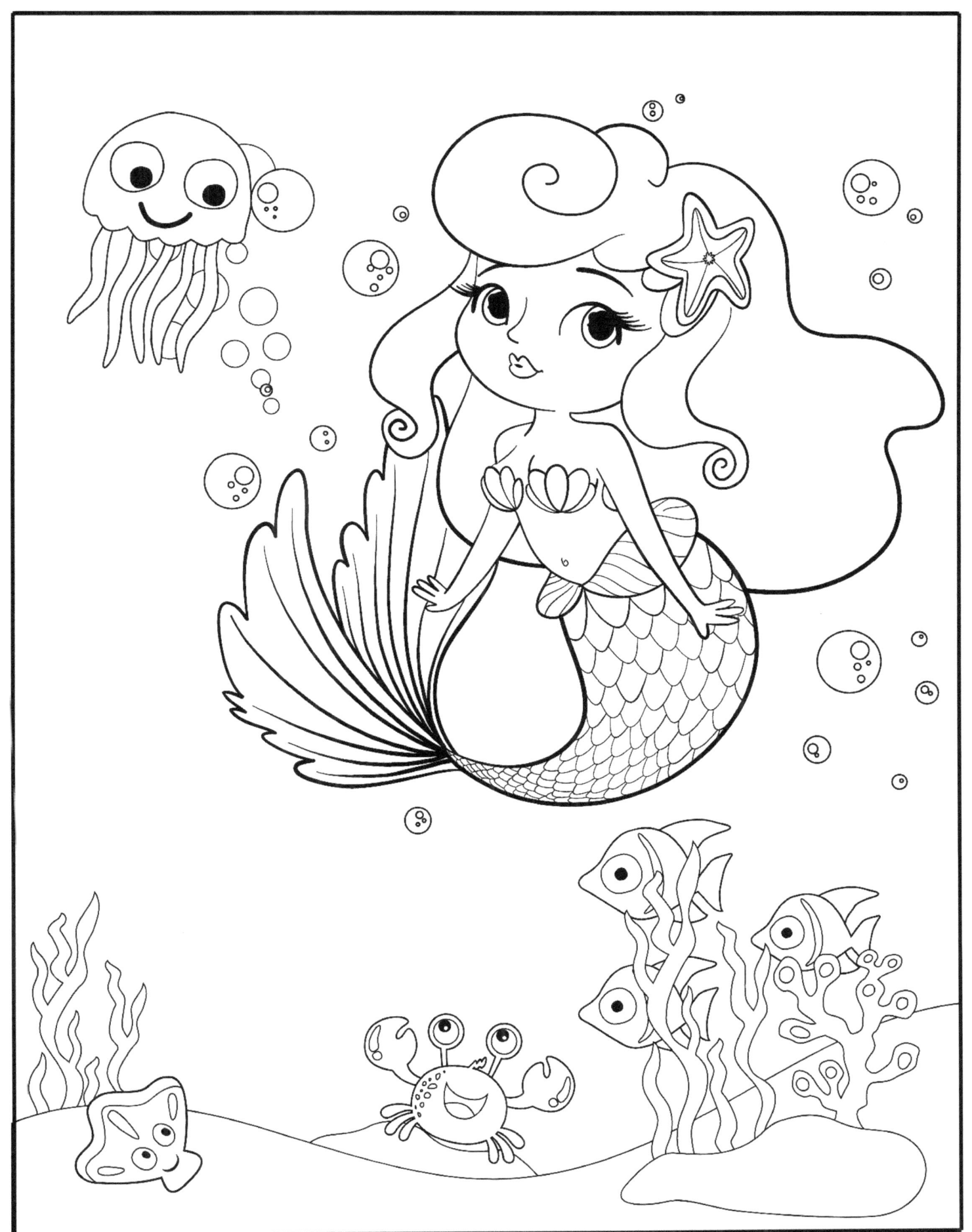

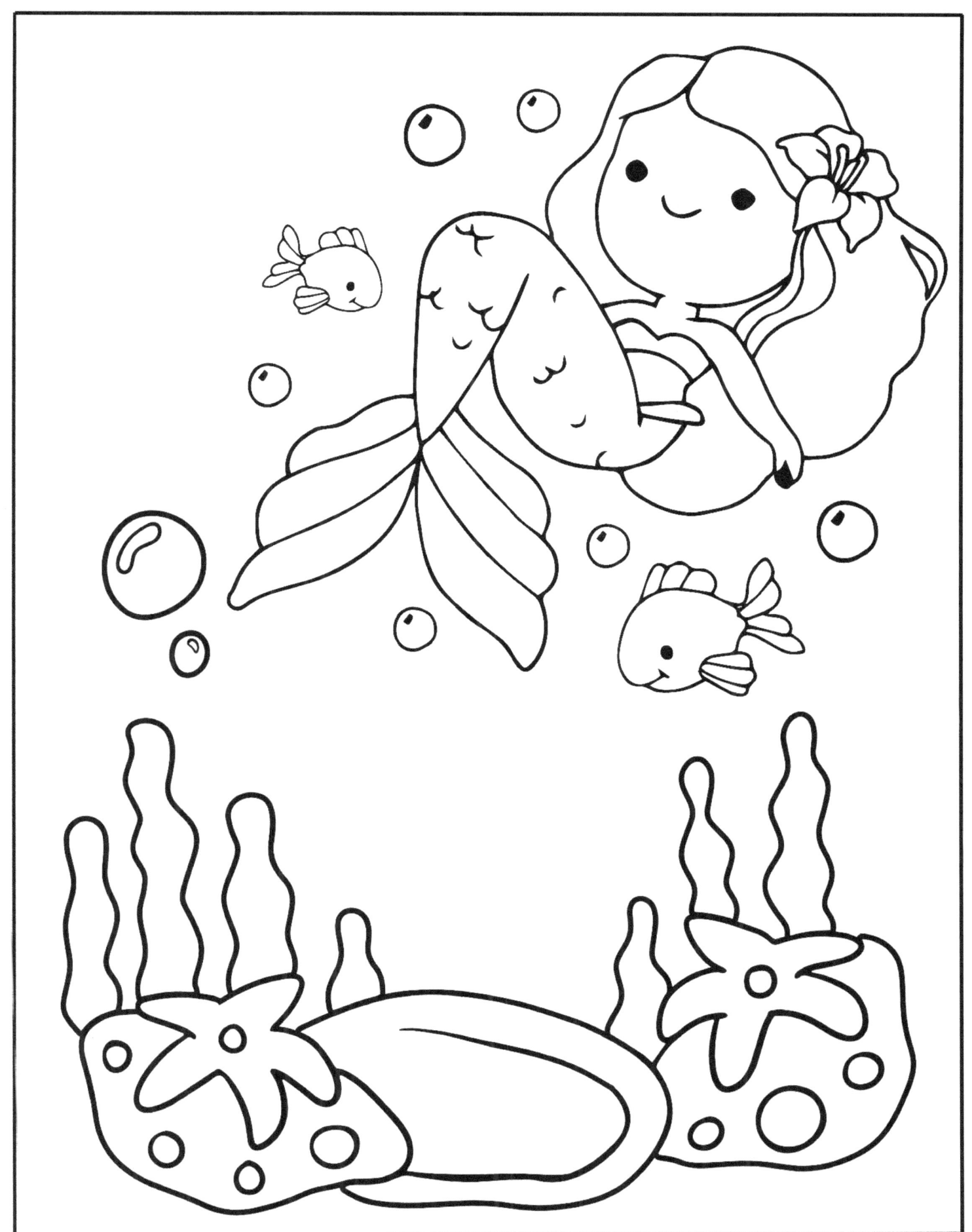

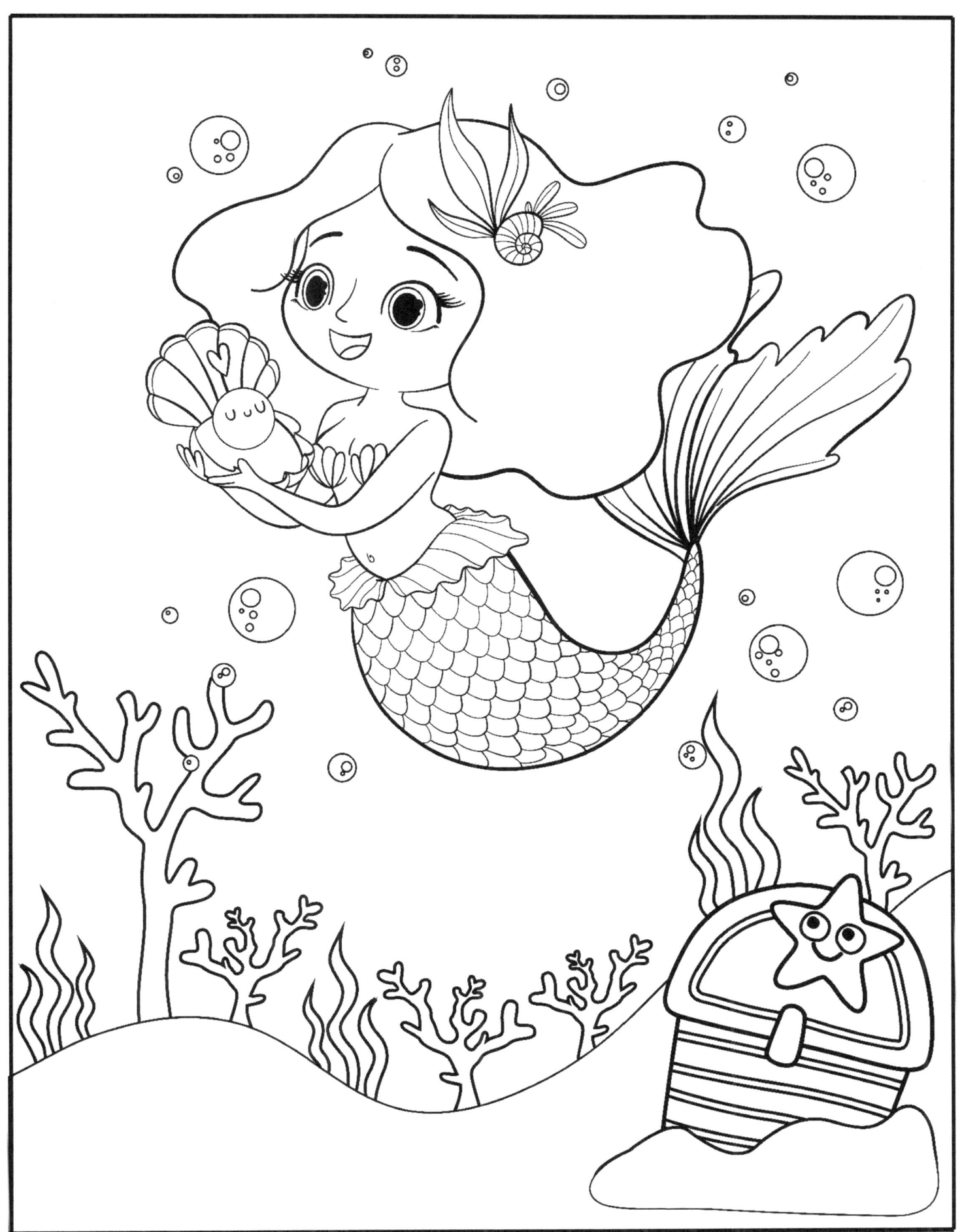

www.ingramcontent.com/pod-product-compliance
Lightning Source LLC
Chambersburg PA
CBHW080614220526
45466CB00010B/3348